21 Day

-

The Real Bluff Creek Story

By
Thom Cantrall

Table of Contents

Foreword

In late September of 1967, two men left their Central Washington homes with a one-ton Chevy truck with stock racks and loaded with horses, fuel and supplies to last them on a trek of over six hundred miles to a remote area of far Northern California in the region of Bluff Creek, Del Norte County. The lure was the report of large tracks, in the range of sixteen inches in length had been reported and these men wanted to know... what was making these huge prints? Could they possibly locate the author of this spoor? They had camera equipment should that happen... but what happened amazed even the pair... and outraged certain unbelieving factions in the world.

An ongoing debate, indeed, at times, a war, was ignited by the short film this outing produced. For nearly fifty years words have been hurled like nuclear bombs at one side or the other. Personalities have been allowed to dominate common sense and real evidence.

In this volume, I intend to wade through the rhetoric and examine the empirical evidence to see if we can arrive at a logical, reproducible conclusion. We shall ignore personalities, allegations and innuendo to examine the facts. Our goal is to determine if that October event really was **21 Days to Destiny** for Roger Patterson and Bob Gimlin...

Part 1

The Stage Is Set…

The View into Bluff Creek

Tom Slick   Dr. Ivan T. Sanderson

Chapter 1-1
1958 – The Jerry Crew Story

The sun had not yet made its appearance this morning in late August, 1958. The stars had faded from their prior glory, but still could be seen here and there to belie the coming heat of a summer day in the mountains of far northern California. Slowly, by threes and twos, the crew building the roads that would facilitate the moving of the vast storehouse of Douglas Fir growing here to the sawmills of the flatland were making their way back to work. It was Monday... and Monday meant they were driving in from town after an all too short weekend at home with family. Most of these men stayed in one camp or another, some down on the paved road where families often joined them on the Klamath River there while others utilized more rustic accommodations found by a convenient wide spot here or there along the stream they knew as Bluff Creek.

It was but the matter of a few moments for those in this weekly migration to drop off the items brought from town to sustain them for the coming week. Some changes of clothes... food, of course and perhaps something liquid to make the nights more sustainable. This task complete, it was on to the job site, now some twenty miles in off the rough pavement of State Highway 96 on a freshly built road that climbs steeply out of the Klamath River basin

Figure 1-1 Jerry Crew

in switchbacks. Past Blue Lake, Beyond the Cooper Ranch, Bee Lake all the way to their equipment and materials storage dump at Louse Camp and more... on they drove until reaching the open dirt that told them they were home... This was their pumpkin patch... the road they were building. Twenty miles is a long way to travel on two ruts in the dust! It was not the work of fifteen minutes and a cup of Starbucks to gain this job... it was more like three times that long and it took a brave (or foolish) man to attempt to drink hot coffee on this route. The chances of wearing that coffee were much higher than ever gaining a taste of it!

Eventually, however, the time came to exit the pickups that brought them in and start up the heavy equipment that would be their home for the next ten hours or more. On this morning, however a surprise was awaiting this gang of experienced mountain people... a surprise of gigantic proportions.

Gerald Crew was a cat skinner for Ray Wallace's construction company who had contracted for the building of the roads into and the logging of a stand of timber owned by the U.S.

7

Forest Service as part of the Six Rivers National Forest and purchased by Block and Company, the prime contractors on this job. On this morning, Jerry, as he was known to all who knew him, walked in the soft dirt track to start his tractor and let it warm up while he did the daily maintenance routine of greasing all the zerks and checking fluid levels on his machine. Jerry was a very experienced and well respected man and had been building roads in this country for long enough to know that the tracks he saw in the soft dirt around his machine where not normal.

The man's first reaction was one of anger. Who in the world was up here playing silly pranks on them by making all these tracks to fool them into thinking something that large had been here? Then he stopped to consider... no one had been here all weekend...

Figure 1-2 D-7 Cat building road

there were no other tracks in the soft dirt of the freshly cut road bed. No one had even stayed in the camps back down the mountain and how would they have gotten here anyway without leaving at least footprints? Jerry called the other members of the crew together and amid the hoots and haws of derision he was hearing from them, others made the same interpretations... these were large tracks and there were no others... no one could even imagine how someone could make a sixteen inch footprint and then walk down the road leaving a trackway with a measured stride of from forty-six to sixty inches? It just didn't make sense to these men that this could be happening.

As a forester, I was taught a method to develop a standard "pacing" step. I practiced this method until it came so second nature to me that I could measure extremely long distances to very close tolerances by pacing the distance and recording the number of steps it took to traverse the distance. My "stride," heel of left foot to heel of right foot in this system was exactly thirty inches. My "pace," heel of left foot to heel of left foot, or a double step, was exactly sixty inches. I have measured distances of over a mile using this discipline and been within a few feet of my goal at the end... often too close to make adjustments. I am 6'4" tall and my "stride" as the term is used here and as Dr. Sanderson used it in his writings, is thirty inches. The being who left that trackway around Jerry Crew's cat had a stride of, nominally, over fifty inches.

Oddly enough, the only crew members not surprised to see this strange trackway were the Indians who were part of the crew. The land they were on was very near both the Hoopa and the Yurok Indian Reservations and many of those men worked on the construction and logging crews in their area. These men just looked at the tracks, smiled and returned to their duties.

It was James Crew, Jerry's nephew and fellow crew member who suggested they follow the tracks to see if they could learn more of his perambulations. It was determined that the subject who left those tracks had not entered the scene on the road, but had descended a very steep slope to the roadway. That mountain slope was determined to be at an angle of seventy-five degrees... a 375% slope... meaning that it rose three and three-quarters feet for every foot it moved horizontally. Believe me, that is steeper than a man would want to walk. The tracks left the slope and proceeded to Jerry's cat where it circled it before proceeding back down the newly cut roadbed. It then cut across the road to the opposite side to the one it had been walking and dropped off another bank stated by Dr. Ivan Sanderson to be steeper than the slope it had descended in attaining the road initially, though how much steeper, I could not imagine.

To illustrate exactly how steep this slope was, do the following. With a piece plain paper, mark a point. From that point, measure horizontally one inch and make another point. Measure vertically for three and three quarters inches and make a third point. Now, simply connect your first point with this third point and the resulting line represents the slope traversed by that creature. Now each of us should ask ourselves how we would do trying to negotiate that grade. In comparison, no Interstate Highway will have a grade exceeding eight percent. No logging road on public land will ever exceed sixteen percent. A normal stairway in a house should never exceed ninety-two percent grade. This slope was almost four times that steep. To match this slope in a step of stairs in a house, the standard steps would be nearly a full YARD above the previous one!

Figure 1-3 Slope

It was stated that the only time the measured stride varied significantly was when an obstacle presented itself to the

10

individual's free travel. The size of the track and the stride reported, by application of the anatomical standard for primates, would indicate an individual of a nominal eight feet and eight inches in height and in excess of seven hundred fifty pounds in weight. That, as one can readily see is larger than any human living.

By this time, the machines were all warmed up and ready to run, so work became the order of the day and the tracks were abandoned, though not forgotten. Talk persisted as to what they could possibly be... what could possibly have made them and discussions of other tracks naturally came up. This was not the only, nor even the first such occurrence of this type. Over the prior years, such things had been reported on a regular basis. Just a few days prior, a report very similar had come from a crew building roads in the Korbel area, just a few miles south of this crew.

More importantly, this was not the last such occasion. This fellow returned on a semi regular basis to inspect the work site, leaving his large tracks in the soft soil to confound and confuse the men working there. Every few days, he would return, only to disappear again and not come back for an interval.

One of the staunchest skeptics among the crew began telling his wife in camp what they were finding on the mountain... at first she just did not believe the stories he was telling her, but as he became more convinced and less skeptical, she became more confused... so much so that in late September Mrs. Jesse Bemis wrote a letter to Mr. Andrew Genzoli, a columnist on the Humboldt Times newspaper in Eureka, California, stating that there was talk all around the job about "Wildmen" living in the mountains of Humboldt and Del Norte Counties and was there any truth to this? Does a wild man really live in these mountains?

Mr. Genzoli stated that he first regarded Mrs. Bemis' letter as a prank but as it lay on his desk, it begin to look more and more interesting, so he finally decided to run it in his column on September 21, 1958. The response was not at all what he expected. Although he did get a percentage of reader's responses expressing hate and vitriol for broaching the subject, the majority of the response was in support of her question and contained many stories from others who had experienced this phenomenon.

Figure 1-4 Jerry Crew with casting

On October second and third, our big footed friend returned to the Ray Wallace job but this time, Jerry Crew was prepared and he used plaster of Paris to make castings of the big guy's tracks. The big guy returned on the fourth as well, but by this time, Mr. Crew had traveled from the job site, it being the weekend, and had taken his track casts to Eureka to show a friend.

Word got to Andrew Genzoli that Jerry Crew was in town

12

with these casts and he invited him to get together to discuss what had been happening. Mr. Crew and Mr. Genzoli met and Jerry even allowed himself to be photographed with his track casts. He did, however, refuse to smile in any of the pictures because he did not want to portray that he might be flippant or less than serious about what he was showing here. Andrew Genzoli satisfied himself that the results of his investigation into Jerry Crew's background was,

Figure 1-5 Genzoli and Crew appear in newspaper article

in fact, true and that Jerry was a non-drinking active member of his church who enjoyed a well-deserved reputation as a sober, reliable and truthful person.

Following this interview, Andrew Genzoli published a feature article that appeared as a headline on October sixth, 1958 in the Humboldt Times newspaper. This article was picked up by the wire services and appeared in newspapers around the world. In this article, Mr. Genzoli called the creature, "Bigfoot", the first time that name was applied to the being in print.

Dr. Sanderson, in his November 1961 report that appeared in "True" magazine stated concerning this event: "...There, (Bluff

Creek, California) enormous footprints turned up night after night all over a new road being bulldozed into a wilderness area not one hundred miles from the town of Eureka. They were inspected by several hard-boiled and highly practical-minded bulldozer operators, loggers and road-engineers and even by press photographers. They were up to twenty-two inches long, appeared night after night out of impenetrable forests, went up impossible slopes, meandered around machinery left parked at night, and wandered off back into the wild with sixty inch strides. They caused a great stir, which prompted some enquiry. This brought to light the fact that such things had been reported off and on for a century all over the area and as far away as Idaho, Oregon and Washington. Further, they linked up with similar sightings in British Columbia."

At the time, this author was fifteen years old and living relatively close to the area in question. My family had friends who lived very near the location and a short few later my own parents were living and operating a business in Willow Creek, California, the hub city for the entire area and home for many of the crew members on the Wallace Brothers Construction Company road building crew. It was this proximity and personal interest that first ignited my interest in this subject, lighting a fire that, while fanned some by my father who had a way of inciting my curiosity, burns even more brightly today that it did all those many years ago. For fifty-seven years now, I have been pursuing this subject all across North America and have been rewarded for this diligence far beyond my wildest 1958 fantasy!

At the time of the incidents related, the company's owner had been away and out of the country. He had been in Costa Rica, Central America assessing the possibility of helping that nation access and harvest some of the very valuable hardwoods species that were indigenous and found in great numbers in the mountainous jungles so prevalent there. Ray Wallace returned to his job site during the second week in October, 1958 to find out all that had been happening in his absence. To say that his job was bedlam would have been gross understatement.

Figure 1-6 Ray Wallace

It is never easy to maintain a crew when working out of a camp environment such as these men were forced to do. Crew turnover rates were high in such situations, but nowhere near what he found when he arrived. It seemed the only men who were remaining calm throughout this were those who had been hired from the Hoopa and Yurok Reservations nearby. The Indians just accepted what was and did their jobs. One of Mr. Wallace's first actions on his return was to get with his brother, Wilbur, also part of the crew, to find out what had been happening.

Wilbur spent hours bringing his brother up to date on the events that had been transpiring in his absence. He told him of the nightly visitations by their large friends... the myriad of tracks he'd left during these visits. Wilbur did his best to convince his brother that what he was relating had actually happened, but didn't appear to be having a lot of luck in doing so. Ray knew the situation they

15

were in... it was fall and time for construction was running out faster than he wanted. They were under contract to finish this job and it was going to be difficult to do so with his crew deserting him over some fanciful stories.

Wilbur was not well pleased that his brother could not accept the facts as he understood them and as he had seen them unfold before his own eyes, so hoped to create more of an effect when he told him of the vandalism that had been perpetrated along with the tracks being left.

First, Wilbur explained, they came to work to find a nearly full fifty-five gallon drum of diesel fuel used in the machinery to be missing. The tracks indicated that the being had picked up the barrel and carried it down the road, crossing to the open side before tossing it one hundred-seventy-five feet from the road in the heavy brush. He noted to his brother that that drum would weigh over four hundred pounds with as much fuel as it contained. Diesel fuel weighs, he reminded Ray, about seven and a half pounds per gallon... less than water, but still most substantial. When Ray wondered if it might have been rolled down the road grade rather than carried, Wilbur explained that there had been no tracks in the soft soil indicating it had been either dragged or rolled... and they would have certainly been evident had they been there. That barrel, he explained had been carried to the point where if could most effectively been thrown over the bank!

On another occasion, Wilbur explained, they had returned in the morning to find a tire off one of their earth mover scrapers, about two hundred fifty pounds in weight, had been carried and rolled for more than a quarter of a mile back toward the equipment dump at Louse Camp before being hurled, not rolled into a very steep ravine... again, the creature had located the spot where it was most effectively released to create the maximum discomfort for those who would have to retrieve it from the canyon bottom. This

16

fact was not well received by the senior Wallace brother and he asked Wilbur if this was all he had to share?

When Wilbur told him it was not, Ray resigned himself to hear more. Although he was not sure of the truth of what he was hearing, he could imagine the deleterious effects it would have on the morale of his crew. Even as Wilbur began his next account, Ray was thinking of some way to counter the negative effects this was having on his crew.

Most recently, Wilbur explained, Jerry Crew had returned to the dump at Louse Camp and found that a section of eighteen inch steel culvert pipe was missing from the stack. This twenty-four foot section of pipe would weigh approximately three hundred and sixty pounds. There were no machine tracks anywhere near that stack and it was clearly gone! It was later found at the bottom of a steep sided ravine approximately a hundred and fifty feet from the road way.

To say that Ray Wallace was not totally convinced would not be an exaggeration at this point, but he left his brother with a new respect for the events of the last six weeks. It was beyond his imagination how someone could have sneaked in and did all that was attributed to these mythical beings, for, after all, that's what they were, weren't they?

It was mark of the times in the 1940s and 1950s that on virtually all roads, any spring adjacent to the road was developed and a trough installed to help motorists along their way should their engines overheat... a very common occurrence in cars of that

Figure 1-7 Print Found in Mud

era. A serendipitous side effect of this was a wonderful place to quench one's thirst with the finest water to be had anywhere and to refill, as needed, the desert bag that depended from the front bumper, cooling the water within through the action of evaporation. Today, that function has pretty much been replaced by Convenience Stores and bottled water that's marketed as "pure spring..." but actually comes out of a well and is, in fact the most polluted water one can purchase due to the greases falling into it from bottling machinery. In the area we are discussing here one such spring tank was to be found not far from the supply dump at Louse Camp. It was here that Ray Wallace stopped on that day in week two of October and found, there in the mud around the tank overflow, masses of tracks... from, as Dr. Sanderson said, Mr. Bigfoot.

At this point, the road builder knew that all that had been told him regarding the events of these past weeks were true. He could no longer remain skeptical or doubtful in the light of this new evidence he knew, because of the sequence of events of this day, could not have been faked or hoaxed for him to find. Mr. Bigfoot did exist... and he did exist on his job site... and he was a major obstacle in the way of completing this project on time.

About this time, another player came into the picture on this remote road site. Ray Kerr from Eureka had heard of the occurrences on this job and was most interested in tracking this creature. Since he was an experienced cat skinner, he was hired immediately with the understanding that he would work a full shift during the day and any tracking he did would be on his own time after his work for the day was complete. As this was Mr. Kerr's intent, he readily agreed. Ray brought with him, however, something more.

Along with Ray Kerr came Bob Breazeale, his wife Leslie, then age thirty five years and Bob's four highly experienced hunting dogs. Bob came with from a hunter's background. He and his dogs had hunted world-wide and his dogs were the envy of all who had seen them work. He carried a "large caliber, English made rifle" that seemed to be to the interest of all those in camp. Bob, Leslie and the four dogs were not hired on the road crew but came along simply to hunt and track. Their seeming goal was to capture or kill one of these "beasts" that were wreaking such havoc on the Wallace Brothers Construction Company's crew roster. The date this began is not certain, but on fifteen October, 1958, Ray Kerr and Leslie Breazeale were riding in Ray's vehicle when Ray spotted a "gigantic humanoid covered in six inch long dark brown hair" crouched by the side of the road.

According to their description of events as reported in a feature article in the San Francisco Chronicle on Tuesday, October 16th, 1958, Leslie Breazeale was dozing in the seat while Ray Kerr was driving. While Leslie did not see the creature initially, Ray did and he reported that it rose from its crouched position to full height and in two steps crossed the twenty foot wide roadway and exited over the bank. The range from the vehicle to the being was approximately forty feet. This occurred within one and a half miles of the Company's supply dump at Louse Camp.

Leslie testified that the action of Ray breaking precipitously woke her from her slumbers immediately and she witnessed the creature as he left the roadway after having crossed in front of their vehicle. Measurements were taken and recorded. The roadway measured twenty feet in width and the being was approximately forty feet in front of where the car was when the brakes were initially applied. The tracks were sixteen inches in length and were very much the same as a human track would be in that same soil, only much deeper and the stride very much longer.

To fast forward a bit here, on seventeen June, 2014, I was on a parallel road to this one about six air miles east northeast of this site and had identically the same thing occur to me and two passengers in my car. On this occasion, there were two sasquatch individuals in the road when I rounded a curve and much the same thing happened. The only thing markedly different was the range from my car to the subjects was about half what it was near Louse Camp that day in 1958. The entire story of this encounter will be found later in this volume.

Bob Breazeale was immediately notified of this occurrence and quickly put his dogs on the trail. He transported them to the

scene and released all four of them together and the left the roadway in hot pursuit and were never seen again. It has been reported that the skin and bones of these dogs were found splattered on trees in the area sometime later, but that has

Figure 1-8 Hunting Hounds

never been confirmed.

With the rapid departure of his hunter and the vaunted dogs, Ray Wallace then resorted to a bit of subterfuge on his own part. Desperate to keep his crew intact, the contractor hit upon the idea of making an over-sized foot of wood and leaving tracks of his own making in an attempt to convince workers that it was simply he and not some mysterious, mythical creature leaving large tracks all over the mountains. It was a sad footnote on an otherwise stimulating series of events in a hidden mountain hideaway. Fortunately, the faked tracks are easily recognized and no tracker of any ability at all would ever mistake them for the real things. The first thing Mr. Wallace learned about making fake tracks with a sixteen inch long and six or seven inch wide prosthesis is that, although his body weight did not change, his area on the ground did, creating the effect of wearing snowshoes. In essence, it was very difficult to leave prints in any but the softest of soils. He simply could not place enough pressure per square inch to penetrate the soil to any extent. This is a dynamic that has faced all who followed

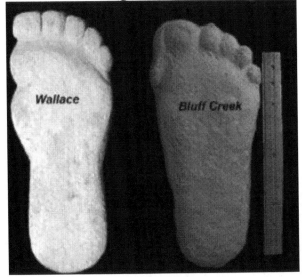

Figure 1-9   Comparison of Wallace Print with Actual Print

who would emulate his endeavor. Unfortunately, there are those who do not know better who continue, to this day, to ascribe to the "fact" that the Jerry Crew prints were made by the owner of the company (an owner who was out of the country at the time) to fool the people in the area.

Even at this early stage of reporting of this phenomenon, the doubters, nay-sayers and haters existed. Andrew Genzoli found out first-hand the results of speaking out on something so unknown as he suffered, in the words of Dr. Sanderson, "brickbats from deniers..." Sanderson went on to decry the attitudes of "educated men" who refused to even hear what was presented on the subject when approached with it. At least, however, that group remained quiet. Dr. Grover Krantz stated that, "If I had the body of a sasquatch in my office I would have to physically drag those

21

scientists into my office and rub their face on the body before they would admit to even having seen it..."

There is, however, one group that has no problem speaking out loudly and in quantity... those who disagree with the idea. These people take many forms and guises. Some are zealously religious and are afraid this information might, somehow, undermine their faith. I have had conversations with this type of person and they seem of two general types.

There is first, the person who denies even the dinosaurs ever existed because, after all, the earth is only five thousand years old because that is when the Bible starts. The second is a bit more pragmatic in that he does admit that dinosaurs were once around, they were just "pre-flood" and somehow (he doesn't explain exactly how) missed the boat. With this fellow, it's the timeline that trips him up.

Now, lest I be thought here to be anti-religious, let me state that I, myself, hold the Priesthood... but I can still think for myself on matters. I understand that there may be many things we don't yet know and act accordingly.

Which brings up the third class of nay-sayer... the "pure science" group. If it is not discovered by "science" and cataloged by them, it cannot exist. These are those who state that observation is invalid... the eye-witness accounts are not acceptable. (I've always found it amazing that my eye-witness testimony can send a person to the death chamber, but it's not acceptable to these people as to the possible existence of a life form...) This person is often heard demanding proof from the person telling what had occurred.

It should be noted that proof is a very personal thing. I cannot prove anything to anyone... I can only offer evidence. It is up to the individual to decide whether that evidence is sufficient to constitute proof in his mind. It is incumbent on those desiring proof that they do more to obtain that proof than watch the latest trendy television on the subject... if one desires proof, one must be willing to go forth and seek that proof. There is one other trait that is even more difficult for me to understand, and that is he who range from total understanding of the existence of this being to those with merely an understanding of that fact but who REFUSE to accept the premise that others may have observed some trait, facet or ability in it that they have not... and that they cannot accept for some reason. It amazes me that people can be so narrow minded as to insist that their understanding of the creature is the ONLY understanding to be heard!

In reading the bibliography provided with this volume, I came across one fact early on... those who are the loudest in their denial of the existence of this being... those who are the loudest in attacking others are those with the least actual experience in the field. I never cease to be amazed by how vicious people can be to one another over something that has not harm in it... to the individual attacking, it really makes absolutely NO difference whether the creature we call bigfoot or sasquatch exists or not... for him, the sun will still rise tomorrow... his mortgage payment will still be due on the tenth of the month... his job will still be there on Monday morning, but he allows himself to be vitriolic in his attacks on others because they have experiences they interpret other than his own.

Chapter 1-2
1959 - 1967   The Intervening Years

In September of 1959 there was a quiet exploration beginning in the California North Coast area. A Texas oil billionaire who had financed four expeditions to the Himalaya region of Nepal in Asia in search of evidence relating to yeti had created a consortium of interested persons who had the money to devote to such a project and a team had been assembled to explore the Bluff Creek area and surrounding environs for evidence of the elusive sasquatch being who reportedly lived there.

Tom Slick, from San Antonio, Texas had recruited Fort Worth, Texas oilman, F. Kirk Johnson who had participated with Slick financially in the 1957 Nepal yeti expedition, C.V. Wood, president of "Freedom Land Organization" in New York City and Wally Heins of the "International Latex Company" also of New York. While the expedition was the brain child of Tom Slick, all four men contributed to the

Figure 1-10   Bob Titmus, l. with castings of prints found

24

financing of this bold enterprise.

The Pacific Northwest Expedition was coordinated by Bob Titmus, a Redding, California area taxidermist who had a great deal of experience in this particular area. Mr. Titmus had participated in the investigations of the Jerry Crew incidents and other reported encounters in the general area and was regarded as a serious and capable team player. Also participating in the earlier stages of the expedition were two Canadian personalities with a deep and abiding interest in the phenomenon. John Green was a newspaperman from Agassiz, British Columbia, Canada and Rene Dahinden from the Vancouver area of British Columbia.

Figure 1-11   John Green, Canadian Newspaperman

Of particular note on this team was Dr. Ivan T. Sanderson, well regarded scientist, biologist and prolific author. Dr. Sanderson had received degrees with honors in such diverse fields of study as geology, zoology and botany. He had headed expeditions to all parts of the world for the British Museum and major universities in the United Kingdom. He had also led expeditions for the Chicago Natural History Museum and the Linnaen Society of London, England.

The Doctor's status as an outstanding author is supported by his list of published works. These include such works as "Animal Treasures, "Living Mammals of the World," "How to Know American Mammals," "Animals Nobody Knows," "Living Treasure" among other titles. His works have appeared as "Book of the Month" selections and on various "Best Seller" lists. His credentials are impeccable and his presence on this team is a statement as to the seriousness of Mr. Slick's desire to conduct a quality investigation.

It was the desire of the Slick Consortium to keep this entire expedition under a strict veil of secrecy. All who participated were required to sign "non-disclosure affidavits" that would ensure that this effort would not become common, public knowledge. The hierarchy of the team was so adamant in this that even the helicopter pilot who was flying in food and supplies to the four camps was required to sign as well.

The undertaking was massive and participants were recruited from several different disciplines to provide a broad spectrum of academic acumen to the task. In the height of the effort, Slick maintained four separate camps in the area, each conducting its own research and utilizing its own personnel.

This expedition was sited here for a very simple reason... the reports of the subject beings in this area went back to the earliest gold seekers of the late 1840s and early 1850s. There were, literally, volumes of reports from usually reliable people with no discernible reason to promote a fantasy and they all centered in this general area.

As recently as the prior April, two fliers, a husband and wife team flying in a private plane and been overflying the Bluff Creek area while the ground was still lying deep under snow at the higher elevations. Many of these ridge tops were rocky and barren and, hence, were bare of trees. The couple stated that they had seen large tracks in the snow and that when they followed this trackway, they finally sighted the creature making them. "It was enormous, humanoid and covered with brown fur," reported Dr. Sanderson in his account of the incident.

There were other reports more easily investigated from the area as well. In one, two doctors reported having encountered a bigfoot on Highway 299, which traverses this area from the Eureka/Arcata area in the west to Redding in the east, a distance of approximately one hundred and forty miles. Another interesting report came from a "lady of high integrity" as she was described by Dr. Sanderson, who, in the company of her daughter, saw two of these beings, "one smaller than the other by far" feeding on a hillside above the Hoopa Valley. Hoopa is a town on the Hoopa Indian Reservation just twelve miles north of Willow Creek on Highway 96. The lady further stated that when she was a young girl, people used to see these creatures from time to time when they went fishing up certain creeks leading into the Hoopa Valley. She stated that she had once seen one swimming across Bluff Creek when it was in flood. She maintained that people did not go above certain points in these valleys because of the presence of these beings. When queried on these points, one Hoopa Indian man of middle age simply asked, "Good Lord, have the white men finally gotten around to that?"

Part of the Pacific Northwest Expedition itself had personal experiences to offer as well. John Green and Bob Titmus had, on August sixteenth, 1959, found bigfoot tracks twenty three miles up the newly constructed road... even past the Louse Camp area. Also found were a great many long, dark hairs that had been located stuck on the trunks of fir trees in the rough, coarse bark common to them. These hairs ranged in length up to about ten inches in length and were found to a height of six feet four inches above the ground. The pair found fecal droppings of extreme size and girth containing fur, small bones and other residues. Dr. Sanderson described the

27

fecal matter as being "as large as that of a twelve hundred pound horse..."

By the winter of 1960-1961, Bob Titmus had assembled quite a noteworthy crew and an equipment yard full of the latest gear to assist in the search. He had amassed four-wheel-drive vehicles as well as some very rugged two wheel drive motorcycles to aid in getting around in this land of very little access. To this end, they had acquired the use of an equipment yard in Salyer's Bar, close to Willow Creek, California. This yard served as the headquarters to as many as four separate remote camps.

For some reason, Slick brought in two brothers he'd worked  with in Nepal on the Yeti expeditions to head up this work in California. This proved to be a terrible mistake as the Byrne brothers had no idea of the problems involved, the

Figure 1-12 Peter Byrne

people involved nor of the quarry involved.

In a personal interview with the newspaperman from Agazziz, BC, Canada, John Green, he related what he perceived as catastrophic mistakes and he and the other main Canadian contingent immediately left the enterprise and returned to his home. I do not believe this animosity, which still exists today, helped in the quest.

In 1962, Tom Slick was tragically killed when his plane crashed. Funding died immediately and the project was terminated.

During these years, many different people tried to develop more information on these denizens of the deep forests. John Green continued his investigations as did Rene Dahinden, Bob Titmus and others. Mr. Green was convinced by this time that the sasquatch of British Columbia, Canada was, indeed the same being as was being found in northern California and proceeded along this line of research. It is interesting to note that almost all of these researchers of this era never saw one of these beings themselves, but had to rely on the results of their investigations to prove to themselves the existence of this being.

It was related by Mr. Green that "the evidence was so compelling and overwhelming, coming as it did from so many diverse sources without benefit of intercourse that it was impossible to not believe such a being had to exist."

The truth is, John Green never had a personal encounter... Peter Byrne never had a personal encounter... Rene Dahinden never had a personal encounter... Bob Titmus did in later life after removing himself to the coastal

Figure 1-13 Rene Dahinden, Canada

sections of British Columbia in the area of Bella Coola where he spent a good deal of his life in this quest.

29

Part 2
Destiny's Doors

Patterson-Gimlin Film

Chapter 2-1

Prelude to a Film

During the mid-sixties, two other persons of note set into motion a set of circumstances that would culminate in the events that inspired this missive.

In 1958, two amateur rough stock rodeo riders happened to meet. Since they both rode bulls and broncs and hailed from the same area of the country, they had a commonality that brought them together and caused a friendship of sorts to grow between them.

Bob Gimlin was born in 1931 in a small town near Branson, Missouri. Bob was of Native American descent, being Chiricahua Apache Indian. Bob, with his family

Figure 2-1   Bull Rider

moved to central Washington about 1940 when Bob was nine years old. The family settled in the Ahtanum Valley very near where Bob resides today. Their ranch was in the area of the vast Yakama Nation Reservation and a huge wild horse herd roamed the sage covered hills between the ranch and the reservation. Bob, as a very young person made considerable money for the time catching and rough breaking these mustangs before offering them

31

for sale at the local auctions. I suggest that anyone who has the opportunity inveigle Bob into telling you his story of how he would catch this wild stock, hook them to a no-longer-used wagon and go tearing across the sage covered wilderness until, often, he ended up with only the tongue and maybe the front axle remaining of the wagon!

After serving in the U.S. Navy during the Korean Conflict from 1950 through 1953 and as a result of this ability to handle rough stock, Bob began a short career in rodeo. It was during this time that he met Roger Patterson.

Roger was a couple of years younger than Bob, being born on Valentine's Day, 1933. He originally hailed from Wall, South Dakota where, legend has it, it is illegal for any male over age of three to appear in public without a cowboy hat and (optional) chaps. Cowboy boots were also required prior to actually walking! Naturally, Roger learned to rodeo as well, and being a smaller built person with a tremendous natural athletic ability, was destined for rough stock work.

As Bob relates the story, he had retired from full time rodeo riding by the end of 1958 and returned to his Yakima, Washington area home to take a more "normal" job. He worked a lot as a truck driver and his bride, Judy worked in a local bank. Bob also kept an active business going on the side breaking and training young horses.

He stated that he was in town one day in the early 1960s, I believe, when he heard a voice call out his name and, turning, saw Roger Patterson coming towards him. Bob was excited to see his old friend and asked how he had been doing whereupon Roger explained that he had been ill... something called Hodgkins disease (a form of Cancer)... but, although he was ill and weak, he seemed to be in remission at the time. Conversation revealed Bob's work with the young stock and when Roger questioned him about this, it

32

turned out that Bob often took the colts right past Roger's place to exercise them and work them on the trails into the Cascade Mountains. Roger asked if it would be possible to just stop by his place and he'd load his pony in with Bob's and they could ride together.

As it turned out, this happened often in those years. And, perhaps prophetically, Roger had developed an interest in the subject of sasquatch... he would bring along a tape recorder and play tapes from people who had had encounters for Bob to listen to in the evening around the fire. Eventually, this expanded further to the two of them riding to likely areas while Roger searched for

Figure 2-2 Mt. St. Helens - Washington State

signs of this elusive hominid.

One of their favorite places was the area around Mount Saint Helens in western Washington. There were many roads and trails in the area and it was a very beautiful place to ride. Bob is quick to

33

tell us he never saw anything here to change his status as a skeptic. In all their wandering, he never found so much as a footprint that he could believe was from a sasquatch.

Bob describes Roger as a "tinkerer"... if he had something mechanical, he would figure out a way to make it better and attempt to change it... often successfully. Roger was also a saddle maker of no small skill.

Roger has often been described by critics as "never working". While it is unsure exactly what that means, it is true that he did not live a "standard" lifestyle, but it would seem that living with cancer would probably be enough to cause one to find alternative ways to make a living.

In late August of 1967, Roger received word that tracks of the sasquatch had been discovered in a remote area near Mount Saint Helens in southwestern Washington and he recruited Bob to carry their horses to the area and they could spend some time riding there to see what they could find. To that end, the pair drove the short distance from their homes to the Saint Helens area with the idea of spending the Labor Day weekend, 1967, investigating the possibility of such a being living there.

The pair, with their stock, was greeted by incessant rain... and one has to experience a storm on the west slope of the Cascade Mountains to truly understand how wet, cold and miserable one can be in a very short time. Eventually, the pair gave up on their search as they could not get off the main roads, even with the horses due to conditions and they finally yielded to common sense and retreated back to the warmer, drier climes of eastern Washington.

Bob related that he had only been back at work for a matter of a few days when Roger stopped by his home to ask if he could drive them with their horses to California. It seems some tracks had been found in a place called Bluff Creek near an unimproved campground called Louse Camp. As will be recalled, this is the same Louse Camp used by the Ray Wallace construction crew as their main equipment dump in 1958.

Bob, who was working for a roofing company in Yakima, Washington as a hot-melt roofer, told Roger that it would be impossible for him to get away just then. He explained that he had stock to tend on the home ranch as well as he had a need to work as much as possible as the roofing season was dying down and they would soon be out of work entirely.

During the last week of September Bob told Roger that it appeared he would be available to make the trip by the end of the month. To this end, Roger put together everything needed to make the trip while Bob continued to work. This included borrowing one horse from a neighbor named Bob Heronimous. Chico was a good, stout roping horse, according to Bob Gimlin and could also be counted on to pack. Both Roger and Bob knew this horse well as Heronimous had used him in some of the work done for Roger prior to this trip.

When all was in readiness, the two men set out on the more than six hundred mile drive from Bob's home to Louse Camp in Northern California, arriving on either 30 September or 1 October 1967.

Chapter 2-2
Bluff Creek Odyssey

California's fall rains, so prevalent in the north part of the state, greeted the two men as they made their preparations for their explorations and discoveries. Unfortunately, this rain destroyed the tracks that had lured them to this area. While they were discernible if one knew what they had been, to Bob, they were merely amorphous blobs, meaningless shapes pressed into the mud.

This began a routine that was to continue for their entire stay... On the horses riding the back country during daylight hours, then in Bob's one ton truck, driving the roads at night in hopes of meeting one of the denizens of this area. The pace was grueling and fatigue was a factor. The two men persevered day after day in their quest... Onion Mountain, Blue Creek Mountain, Forest Road 15... Forest Road 12... if there was a road, they traveled it... Turtle Rock, Nikowitz Peak and the Siskyou Range were their home for this period.

Sightings were common of the animals that resided there... Bears, Cougars and deer were seen regularly. Bobcats, skunks and the myriad small critters were everywhere but there was not one instance of anything that could have been Sasquatch to be found in all their perambulations.

Trips were made the thirty miles or so to town for gas

regularly. They had spare cans they filled to minimize the number of trips they had to make as this was a monumental waste of time for them.

For twenty days, this routine prevailed... ride and drive... search and hope until, on the evening of the twentieth day, Bob told Roger that it was time to point back north. He explained that he had things to get done before winter set in and it was time to be

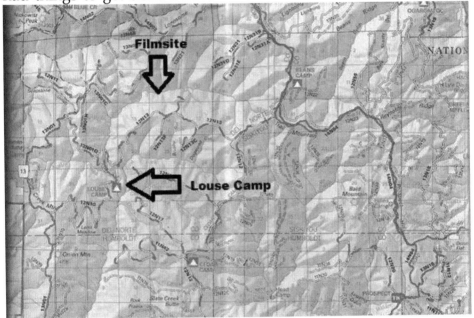

Figure 2-3 Bluff Creek Environs

about them. It was a Thursday evening when this occurred and as much as Roger tried to change Bob's mind, it was not going to be... Bob was headed home after the weekend.

"Okay," Roger commented, "What would you think about leaving me here and coming back to get me after a while?"

"Roger," Bob replied, "that is not going to happen. If I leave you here, you are going to be here until spring because I am not coming back!"

"Well, since we only have a few more days, how about we take a pack horse and go up into that good habitat area we saw the other day?" Roger continued, "We can stay overnight there a couple of nights and be back in time to load up and get out of here by the end of the weekend."

The agreement made, the pair made ready for a morning departure but Roger, not being ever mistaken as an "early riser" was a bit behind time when they finally left their base camp at Louse Camp. It was the 21st Day... a day of Destiny for these two men and the world at large.

The Encounter

"What did you get on the film?" the man holding the rifle asked of the cameraman. "It looked good from here."

"I really don't know if I got anything," a discouraged Roger Patterson answered as he looked toward the western ridge to judge the time. "I ran out of film and I had to chase it clear across that flat. I fell down coming out of the crick, so I don't know if the danged camera even worked after that."

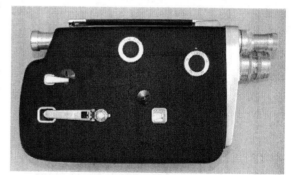

"I saw you fall," Bob answered. "I think I'm going to ride up the crick a ways and see if I can see where it went."

"No, Bob, please don't leave me alone. We don't have any idea if

Figure 2-4 Kodak Manual Film Camera

those other two are still here of if they have gone away. They don't seem to be dangerous... that one certainly wasn't at any rate."

"Stay here with me," Roger continued, "and let's see if we can make some casts of some of these tracks."

Figure 2-5 Roger Pouring Casts

The two men did that. In the afternoon sun, they mixed plaster and poured it into the deep impressions left in the sandy soil of that bar alongside Bluff Creek that Friday in October so many years ago. While the plaster was drying, Bob compared the tracks of his horse to those of the creature they had just watched walk away from them so nonchalantly a few minutes prior. It amazed him that his horse who weighed more than a half ton did not leave impressions nearly as deeply as had that creature they had just watched. Bob even tried jumping from a stump with his high-heeled cowboy boots on to see if he could simulate in any way, the depth of track the hairy beast had made. Try as he might, Bob's best efforts were dismal when compared with those left in the soil. He walked across the sandbar following the trackway and was amazed by the fact that, as casually as that thing had strolled from their view, the stride nearly doubled when it was no longer in their sight. He followed the tracks as far as the creek and found no more than wet spots on the rocks of the stream, apparently indicating where she had crossed the stream and climbed the steep ridge opposite them.

It was the work of some hours to complete their tasks here this day and retreat towards their soogan at Louse Camp at the mouth of Notice Creek on the newly cut road. This camp had been their home for three solid weeks now as they had determined that this was the base of operations that would provide them the best chance of success in their venture... The sun was well down in this

39

late October sky, nearly four pm, actually, by the time the two men reached their camp. Darkness was near by the time the saddle horses and pack horse had been stripped, wiped down and made

Figure 2-6 Frame 354 of the PGF

ready for the night. The two men then loaded into Bob's one ton dually Chevy truck and headed into town.

Most of the thirty plus miles from Louse Camp out over Onion Mountain and down to Highway 96 that took them south toward the town of Willow Creek was done in the gloaming but it was full dark when they finally arrived in the town. That it was the first time that either of the men had been out of the mountains for any reason, other than for gas, in the past three weeks was noticed by no one. Roger and Bob looked up the man that had given them the clue that had led them into these mountains those weeks before.

In early September, Al Hodgson had sent word to Roger Patterson at his Yakima, Washington home... a trackway had been found in the area. Roger immediately went to his saddle partner,

Bob Gimlin to try to enlist him in quest for film sufficient to make a documentary on the legendary Sasquatch. As it turned out, Bob and Roger had just returned from a Labor Day weekend trek into the rain-soaked environs of Mount Saint Helens and, when Roger attempted to recruit Bob, he was told that at the moment, Bob could not get time off his job as a hot melt roofer for a Yakima roofing company. In fact, it was the last days of the month before that became possible and the trip could proceed. Bob had left it to

Figure 2-7 Al Hodgson

Roger to arrange the horses they'd need and he outfitted his truck with all the fuel, etc. necessary for an extended stay in the mountains... a stay that turned out to be approximately three weeks.

On that fateful Friday afternoon of 20 October 1967, about three and one half miles from the bridge over Bluff Creek at Louse Camp, these two men rode out of myth and into Destiny. Bill Munns has described it as the minute of film that has sparked forty seven years of controversy.

It was midafternoon before the riders reached their destiny...

Roger was in the lead followed closely by Bob about a horse length behind and him leading their pack horse with their gear. As they advanced up the sand and gravel banks left behind after the 1964 northern California floods, they approached a log laying in such a way that the upraised root wad had caused the stream to reroute around it, causing an unusual bend in the creek with a berm of sand built up on the opposite side from the fallen giant.

Figure 2-8 Bluff Creek Showing Creature, Log Jam and Bank Where Roger Tripped

As first Roger, then Bob cleared the exposed roots, there stood, directly in front of them at a range of only a few yards a large, hair covered, bi-pedal primate more than seven feet tall and weighing in excess of six hundred and thirty pounds! When the two men first saw her, she was standing and merely watching them approach, making no real effort to escape.

Immediately, Roger grabbed for his hand wound movie camera. His horse, however, had a totally different idea of how this scenario should go down and immediately went into a wild fit of bucking and pitching wildly. Roger was doing his best to clear his mount with the Kodak camera as his colt went to the ground, feet flailing. Being the athlete he was, Roger escaped his dilemma and ran for the edge of the creek and the waiting sasquatch.

Bob's horse was a bit more stable, though it took both hands to control the jittery, nervous mount. To better facilitate this, Bob

42

and his pack horse parted ways, allowing the man to concentrate on what was happening with his pony and the creature in front of him. He watched intently as Roger started his camera while moving toward the creature.

In crossing the creek, Roger's attention was, of course, riveted on the being we have come to know as "Patty", so named by the Russian Humanoid expert, Dimitri Bayonov... In his attempt to negotiate the sand berm beside the stream, Roger tripped and fell on his forearms and knees. It took him only moments to regain his standing position but, by this time, Patty was moving slowly away from the scene of the initial encounter. Quickly, Roger moved across the gravel bar to a position where he could see the large being more clearly and without interference between them. When he achieved a spot that seemed to work for him, he called to Bob, still across the stream, "Cover me!"

On hearing this request, Bob rode his horse across the creek to a spot very near Roger, pulled his 30'06 rifle from its scabbard on the saddle and dismounted the horse to be more readily able to defend them should this being become dangerous. Further, since they had initially been drawn here by the discovery of three sets of tracks of different sizes and seemingly from different family members, it was feared that the other two may still be in the area.

It was when Bob dismounted with his rifle that the large creature turned and looked back at him. It is this famous turn that has been immortalized in the widely known but misnamed, "Frame 352." In actuality, it's Frame 354, but a miscount early on has mislabeled it for all these years! Once Bob had dismounted with his weapon, he simply stood and watched her walk away as Roger did his very best to get film of the enigma...

When she had finally disappeared from site and Roger had walked back to Bob's side, Bob suggested that he ride after her to see where she went but Roger was still spooked by the possibility

43

of there being two more if these individuals as well as the fact that it was late enough in the day by now to make it critical that they get retrieve their missing stock, return to camp for the gear and supplies they'd need to cast some of the tracks left in the sand of this bar.

Roger reloaded his camera with a fresh roll and, as the pair worked the rest of the daylight away, he recorded the scenes generated in the process...

Chapter 2-3
In Bob's Own Words

Following is a description in Bob's own words of the events of that day, October twentieth, 1967... the Day of Destiny... No corrections have been made to his words, it is as he said it, carefully transcribed from an

Figure 2-9 Film Site

oral presentation Bob did a very few years ago.

"...I left out early. I always got up early... Roger didn't. He usually slept in a little more than me. I'm kind of a farm boy so I got up about daybreak every day and saddled my horse and I'd ride out. Well, my horse loosened up a shoe so I rode back in to tighten... to get the equipment to tighten the shoe back up and get it going. Roger came in just a little bit later and he said, 'By golly, Bob being as your gonna go in a few days here, can we go out and stay all night up in the mountains in some of that area where it really looked like great habitat?'"

"I said, 'Well, yeah, I suppose.' So we started out that afternoon, well, it was early afternoon... it suppose it was twelve... twelve-thirty... something like that. (We) took a little horse with us with our sleeping bags and our equipment all on it... rode up this creek bed about three and one half miles from where we were camped... Came around a bend by the crick where there was a ... I don't know how many folks here understand when I say downfall tree. There was a tree downfall with the roots system up. It was probably eight to ten, twelve feet high and that had caused the crick to reroute itself and go around there. I'm not real good on diagrams... Anyway, when we came around that bend in the creek, the creature stood across the crick about as far as far as that gentleman is right there with the paper in his hand (indicating a very close encounter). It was standing when I saw it. It may have been stooped down when Roger first saw it, but I was just a horse length or so behind Roger, leading the pack horse. When I saw the creature it was standing up looking across the crick to where we were. But, it immediately turned and started walking away... just taking natural steps. I mean natural looking steps to us which measure out forty-two to forty-eight inches from heel to toe... which is a pretty good step. There are some pretty tall men here and I'd almost dare them to make a step comfortably that long and keep on walking.

"That's how this film footage kinda got started. Roger's little horse kinda threw a little... I don't know what kind of dance you'd call it, but he wasn't... Roger was trying to bail off and get his camera at the same time... which he did. Roger was a very agile man... of course, he was a rodeo cowboy and he was a great athlete. So he bailed off that little horse, with his camera and ran across the crick trying to get that camera focused on the creature.

There was a little incline of sand alongside the crick on the other side. Roger kinda stumbled and fell when he got on the other side of that. He went down on his elbows. If you've seen that film footage from beginning to end, you'll see all that shaky part at the beginning. There is hardly... you can't hardly identify anything. Then Roger realized the creature was moving on and all this time I was setting right where I was. I stopped... the pack horse pulled loose or I let him go, I don't know. Everything happened so rapidly. I really don't remember if he pulled loose of if I just threw the rope back at him 'cause I was having a little hard time holding my horse. It was an older horse... it was an old roping horse and he was a little bit easier to handle than Roger's little horse that had a lot of spunk."

"There's when it all started going kinda wild. Roger wanted to relocate because she was movin'... I say she but I didn't know if it was a female or a male... it didn't make any difference, it was going, you know? Roger had to relocate to get a better... a better view, so he asked me if I would cover him. He told me later that he never... he was kinda concerned about two more being right close to this one. It was a wooded area on the far side... a really wooded area and you couldn't see up in there so that's what his concern was. Well, I didn't know that but he said 'Bob, will you cover me?' Well, I know I had a rifle in my scabbard on my saddle but I knew I couldn't do it sitting on a horse if anything happened that I needed to do because I was an avid hunter at that time and shot a lot of big game. I knew what I had to do, so I rode across the crick, stepped off the horse with my rifle in my hand... and that's where you see that famous turn when she turns and looks back at me... when I stepped down off that horse."

"Maybe the misconception was that I intended to shoot this creature... I did not intend to shoot the creature. I never raised the rifle to my shoulder... ever. I was carrying a 30'06... a Remington

47

.30'06 with 180 grain bullets in it. I felt if I had to I probably could stop this creature if it came back at us. As long as she kept walking away, I had no reason to even bring the rifle up. Like I said a few seconds ago, everything was happening so rapidly you just didn't have to do a lot. She was walking away all this time. Then, Roger hollered at me, he says 'Damn, Bob, I ran out of film...'"

"I got back up on the horse, I said, 'I'm going to follow...' and he said, 'no... no, no, no, no, no... Bob, don't do that, the other two might be here...' So he was assuming this creature had... we were only about four miles from where those footprints (Thom: these footprints mentioned here are the prints that drew the pair to Bluff Creek to begin with... there were three sizes of prints found there...) were... Roger was assuming there would be two more there and he didn't want to be left there with just a camera in his hand... and no film in it. I mean now it seems kind of amusing to us but I don't think it was to Roger... when I seen the look on his face he was glad I turned around and came back."

"By then, he got under a poncho. I didn't know much about cameras or anything... got underneath an old poncho that I had on the back of my saddle and got more film in his camera. Then we proceeded to catch up his horse which ran down the crick a ways and the little pack horse. And then we tried to follow where this creature went. We got up there a quite a little ways and we only saw one half of a wet print on a rock going across the crick and up the side of the mountain. It was steep and I kinda wanted to go after it, but I didn't know really why, I just wanted to see it again."

"Roger said, 'No, we gotta get back, Bob. Cause October twentieth your days are pretty short down there in the mountains.'"

"When that sun sets over them hills it don't take long 'fore it gets dark. By then, it was in the afternoon and we had to go back down to camp to get the material to make the casts. We did some things there."

"Roger had me get up on a stump about, oh, three and a half or four feet high maybe... that was alongside of where she went and made her tracks. I had on a cowboy boot with a riding heel which is a pretty sharp heel now if you understand what that means. At that time I was a little heavier than I am now... I weighed about one hundred and seventy five pounds. I'd jump off beside this footprint... tracks... with that heel with one foot hit first and see how deep I could go into the soil that she walked through. It wouldn't go near as deep as her tracks were."

Figure 2-10   Bob Gimlin 2010

"Then I rode this horse alongside. He was a sixteen hand quarter horse and he weighed about twelve hundred pounds. With my weight on him and the saddle I rode him right as close without disturbing the tracks as I could. Roger took pictures of that. The horse never made tracks as deep as the creature did. So that indicated right there that she was fairly heavy... that she was a heavy, heavy muscled creature which you can see in all this. "

"People say, 'What'd she weigh, Bob?'"

"I don't know I thought three or four hundred pounds was really big, you know? I said, 'probably three or four hundred pounds and, and six and a half foot tall.' Well, come to find out, I was way off on everything, you know? But, like I say, when I first saw her I was up on a horse sixteen hands high which I was about nine feet up. Things will look a little different from that height."

"...You folks see what the result was from that film footage...

that short film footage that we were lucky enough to get. At that point in time being as Roger fell down, we had no idea that we had any good film footage at all. Naturally we got the cast made and the pictures made of what we had to do there for what evidence we could get. Then we went in to mail that to Yakima or wherever he mailed it to. There has been a lot of controversy on where that film was processed and where it was mailed to. I never paid that much attention to it because I was very tired from being down there three weeks, riding horses every day long hours and driving the truck at night."

"Roger slept in a whole lot better than I did 'cause I just didn't sleep that much down there."

Chapter 2-4
Departure From Destiny

Now, the film, such as it was, was in the can. The two men had hustled into town to meet and talk with Al Hodgson about what they had seen and what they had, hopefully, filmed. Al allowed that he would like to be able to get to the spot, but his duties with his business would not allow it for a time, so Bob took several cardboard boxes to use in covering the individual tracks until he could get there to see them, as he and Roger were leaving the next day for Yakima and home.

About three am, it started to rain lightly and Bob thought about rousing Roger so they could get done what they had to do at first light, get loaded up and get out of there fairly early. Roger was not so easy to rouse however and simply insisted that it would not rain. Just before daylight, the rain began to come down more seriously and things were getting pretty soaked around camp. At this point, Bob insisted that Roger rise and, he determined to return to the film site and do what he could there to preserve it.

When Bob went to get his boxes he'd brought home from Willow Creek and Al, he found them soaked through in the now driving rain. Roger kept insisting that the rain would stop... that it never rained much there... though how he thought that sandbar he'd filmed on the day before had been created, I have no idea... finally, Bob just mounted up and was headed up the creek when Roger joined him. Bob was alarmed even in this short time by how much the creek had risen.

On arrival, he decided his cardboard would not work, so he stripped bark off the dead and dying alders that were there and used those bark slabs to cover the trackway as best he could. With increasing alarm, the two men did as much as they could to preserve the site, then mounted up and headed back to Louse

Camp in a deluge as only northern California can provide when she wants to do so.

As soon as they got back to camp, Bob realized the trouble they were in. The water had risen to an alarming level. The roads here were not rocked.

Figure 2-11 Creek in Full Flood

They were fresh cut and open dirt. As such they were soaking up water at an alarming rate. Bob's truck, while it was a dual rear wheel vehicle was not a four wheel drive truck. Bob told Roger to get the stock gathered up... that he had to get the truck across the creek onto higher ground or it would be there 'til spring. Bob then used all the driving skill he had to ford that raging torrent that, so few hours before, had been a gentle stream... Roger and he then got the stock across and loaded... they then returned to tear down what remained of their camp, load it up and get moving out of there.

Bob's first concern was the climb out of Louse Camp at an elevation of twenty four hundred feet over the summit of Onion Mountain at an elevation of well over four thousand feet. Before they got to the grade, Bob realized they were not going to make it over the mountain and voiced this concern to Roger... Immediately, Roger replied, "Take the lower road..."

Prior to this moment, Bob had never heard of any "Lower

Road"... it had always been climb out over the top of Onion Mountain when they were headed in that general direction. But, realizing what was to happen, he made the turn immediately and proceeded along it cautiously until, shortly, they came to a mud slide. The slide, at this time, covered all but about three feet of the roadway... not nearly enough room for the truck with its load of horses and camp gear to get around.

Bob stopped in the driving rain and got out to look at the depth of the mud, with an idea of driving thru it if possible... what he found was a pile of mud over three feet deep on the shallow end out in the middle of the road. What was up against the bank was deeper

Figure 2-12 Muddy Road

than his truck was high. He determined then that this route was impossible and they were consigned to Onion Mountain or nothing at all. Before getting back into his truck, Bob looked over the situation to see how best to proceed with backing out of there.

Just behind them a short distance was a spot he determined he could effect a turn around with the truck, but getting there was going to be precarious... the creek side was not but a sheer drop off of some twelve to fifteen feet vertical. To insure a level of safety, he stationed Roger behind him to stop him if he got close to that precipice. Returning to the truck, Bob started backing... slowly... when he realized he couldn't see Roger. He continued on very slowly, worried about where the right rear of the truck was in relationship to the drop. Finally, he could stand it no more and he stopped. On climbing out of the cab, he looked for Roger and not seeing him he walked to the rear of the truck where he looked at the situation... his rear duals were within INCHES of the edge of that vertical drop... and Bob nearly fainted when he saw how close it had actually been... He immediately called for Roger and he answered from a ways away... he was standing staring vacantly up the mountain and when Bob began to build up to a chastisement of him, Roger said, "Look... those trees are sliding down the mountain at us..."

Bob did look... and what he saw turned his blood cold... he immediately told Roger to guide him into that wide spot so they could turn around and get the hell out of there! Within a few moments, they had the truck turned and the slide engulfed the entire road where they had been.

In a few minutes the men were climbing up Onion Mountain. The rain was falling so hard the wipers could not keep up and the fresh cut road was now a sea of mud. It was only a few minutes of this until the truck, being two wheel drive could go no more. If anything, the men were in even more dire straits. They couldn't go forward and, when they attempted to go back, the truck slid to the side and the loading ramp that was behind the driver smacked into a tree and held the rig fast in place. This was it... they could not move forward... they could not move back and the rain, if anything, was getting heavier.

In trying to think of a way out of this predicament, Bob remembered that there was some road equipment at the top of the grade, so he took off walking up the muddy trace to see if he could find a help to their situation. What he found was, indeed several machines including a backhoe that had the keys left in it. A drug culture not having found its way into the far mountains yet, it was still common practice to leave the keys in equipment. I even did it in my truck because one never knew when someone would come along and need to move your rig so they could get through. Of course, that is not even to be thought of today.

Bob was familiar enough with a backhoe to realize that it would need help to attain the traction necessary to get them out of their predicament. To help this, he loaded the bucket as full with stones as he could get it... he then returned to his stuck truck where he put Roger under the steering wheel with instructions that, as soon as he had it moving to put into low gear, put the gas pedal to the floor and KEEP IT THERE until they were out! Bob then began maneuvering the tractor into a position where he could provide an impetus to get his rig free. In so doing he put a dent in the hood of that truck that was still in it as late as last year when it was sold from its place of rest in a neighbor's field.

It took time, but, with his tractor providing power and Roger steering and thrusting as much as he could, they reached a point where they could get along on their own, so shut down the tow and returned the backhoe to its place and started on out further. The rain had not abated... in fact, it was so intense and cold, that on his return to the truck from the backhoe, Bob was in the beginning stages of hypothermia and his hands were too cold to be usable. It was necessary that he put them directly on the exhaust to get them warm enough to be able to function sufficient that he could grip the steering wheel.

Shortly after leaving behind the backhoe, another grade was met that had to be negotiated... the mud was no less miserable and, in climbing the grade, Bob started feeling the slogginess that usually indicated a flat tire. "Oh my gosh," he said, "this is all we need, a flat dual... Roger, would you open the door and stand on the running board so you can see and tell me if I have a flat on that outside dual? It feels like it to me..."

Roger did just that... he opened the door and stepped out

onto the running board while hanging out far enough to see... "Bob," he stated with is face as white as a piece of unlined paper, "whatever you do don't stop... don't even slow down... go as fast as hell... that road is falling off into the canyon as we cross it... don't, for heaven's sake, even think about slowing..."

Bob didn't... he revved it more and ran for it... finally crossing out of that mud. The rain did not slack, but at last they reached Highway 96 and Bob turned north for Yakima. It was dark by now, but that didn't matter. Roger assured Bob that he would help him drive and they'd get home, whereupon, he curled up in the cab and went to sleep. And they did just that... Bob drove them home while Roger slept the entire trip in the now warm cab through a dark and rainy night...

As told to Thom Cantrall by Bob Gimlin on Tuesday 2 September 2014 in Ahtanum, WA.

Part 3
And Then...

Frame 354 REAL

Morris & Heronimous Fake

Chapter 3-1
The Aftermath

The two investigators, Roger Patterson and Bob Gimlin, had no sooner arrived home than the controversy began. To begin with, a close relative of Roger had fronted the cost of travel on this expedition and taken control of the resulting film. At a Sunday, October twenty second viewing of the film, he announced that they would be touring from theater to theater with this film, charging admission for it.

When asked about the seeing the film for the first time, Bob stated, "To be truthful, I wasn't impressed. I had seen that creature a lot better than that film showed her..."

Plans were made to tour with

Figure 3-1 Bob Gimlin

the film and Bob even went to Hollywood to meet with film producer David Wolper. Some contingencies were discussed with little actually materializing but the team continued the tour of the film while Bob Gimlin returned home to his family and work.

The team even offered the film to various anthropology

departments at some major universities and the general response was, "Sasquatch is a myth, therefore, any film purporting to show a sasquatch would have to be a myth as well..." and stated they were simply not interested in even looking at it. Amazing the narrow mindedness of some classes of people... Dr. Grover Kranz stated that, "If I had a body of a sasquatch in my office, I would have to drag my associates into the office and rub their faces in it before they would even admit they'd seen it..."

Figure 3-2 Roger Patterson

A substantial amount of money was earned in the tour, although it was not all conducted on the up and up... it is reported that, in Arkansas, at least, an actor was hired to portray Bob onstage in introducing the film... I don't know how he was introduced, but Bob, himself reports having received a phone call from a friend in that area reporting that he was in attendance and a fellow had just been introduced as Bob... it is further reported that the person notifying Bob rather loudly proclaimed that was NOT Bob Gimlin... that he knew Mr. Gimlin personally and this was not him...

he was said to have been escorted from the hall.

Bob did not long participate in the show with the film and, in fact, sold his interest to Rene Dahhinden of BC, Canada for a meager sum. Bob's wife was an employee in a local bank and was receiving tons of pressure over this film and the reports surrounding it. She was being coerced into denying anything to do with it at the risk of her job.

Much has been made of a "Deathbed confession" from Roger when his cancer could no longer be denied in 1972. People have made much of this... even to suggest that Roger denied the veracity of the film, which is wholly untrue... Not at any time did Roger Patterson ever represent that film as anything other than what it appears to be... a bi-pedal, homonid walking across a riverine sandbar in plain sight.

Bob stated that he, when he heard how ill Roger had become, went to see him one last time. In Bob's own words, he explains the conversation, "Roger said to me, 'Bob, I know you haven't had much of a financial gain from all of this, but I have an idea. As soon as I get better and can get out of here, we're going back down to that area we were in California and we'll build a trap and capture one of them. I know we can do that then there will be no doubt left and it will make us rich too.' Of course, he never left the hospital that time... in fact he died just a few days later... but he never stopped believing in what he had filmed and he knew there was more that could be done..." - Bob Gimlin to Thom Cantrall 2 September 2014, Ahtanum, WA

Simultaneously, there arose those who, for one reason or another, were personally challenged by the concept of a large, unknown, bi-pedal primate living in the remote areas of our country and proceeded to launch a war of vitriol against those who believed there could be truth in the stories. Unfortunately this still goes on today.

The introduction of that minute plus of film has ignited a conflagration well beyond anything that might have been considered reasonable. It has made many people lose their perspective on reality and respect. There is no reason for such violent attacks on others because they simply believe this way or that way. I mean, what real difference does it make to the average person among us if this being is real or not? Yes, it is nice to know they are there, but what if they were not? Would it make any real difference in our world? Would the sun fail to rise tomorrow if he exists... or doesn't exist? None of this is true... nothing would be upset... no religions would be proven true nor false and no meals would be lost by anyone.

That said, what is the truth about the film? Those who argue it tend to make statements that, true or not, are picked up parroted by others who feel the same way. These people have no idea if what was said is a fact, it just sounds good and matches what they think and are trying to convince others. Most often, they cannot even cite the source for the statement they are parroting... "I heard someone say..." is a common mantra... "Dr. X said..." is much less commonly quoted.

What would be the result if we were to examine the subject while heeding only the statements of experts in fields under question? Suppose we listened only to the opinions of people who should know that of which they speak? To that end, we are going to examine this film in detail. "My brother-in-law said..." will not be admissible evidence in this court.

One thing that must be made clear from the outset, we cannot, nor do we intend to prove anything to anyone. Anything can be argued honestly or falsely depending on the person presenting the argument and his reasons for doing so. The very best we can ever do is present evidence for our case. Any statement made, picture displayed, video shown serves one purpose only. It offers evidence to support the claims of the person doing the sharing. Of course, the clearer the statement, the more esteemed the author or the more credible the subject, the stronger the evidence becomes.

When a discussion begins and statements are made, it is most important to demand that any statement made as a representation of fact be substantiated by a reference to the person making that statement. Believe, please, in a court of law, "everybody knows..." or "my buddy says..." is not going to be allowed nor should it be allowed in this discussion either. The corollary of that is also true in that both sides of the argument must be prepared to so support their own points of argument.

All too often, the skeptics does not care about the source or the veracity of the author of the statements he represents, therefore, it is essential that this requirement be made known up front. Do not allow such statements to be considered and let the individual know that this is not acceptable in this sense.

If personal opinion is expressed, make sure it is clear that it is opinion then determine how that speaker is qualified to make such a statement. Does he have research time in the field? Has he spent hours in the field investigating the subject at hand? Where did he come by this experience? Is he trained in this field? Does he understand the natural world in the area in which he is offering his opinion? What is the sum of his personal experiences as pertains to this statement? In the realm of personal opinion, it is essential to know how much research time does he have on the subject under question. Exactly what are his personal experiences and where were they that would make them appropriate and relevant to this discussion?

As an example, one of the things I often discuss is the question of the amount of oxygen generated by trees. I can find a plethora of people with opinions, but very few are foresters, agronomists, dendrologists, botanists or even forest ecologists. They have no shortage of opinion on the subject, but few have the technical expertise or scientific training to even begin to understand the ecology of the forest biome.

It is absolutely essential to understand that argument is totally useless with these people. First, in all cases, when the voice rises, reason departs.   One can only discuss these facts with reasonable, logical, open people... to do otherwise flies in the face of reality.   When confronted with such a situation, merely state that you do not have time for spurious argument, but if your antagonist would wish to speak from factual statements not hearsay and innuendo, you would be willing to accommodate them. Remember, only a percentage of the public is thus capable. Most have no experience in any of the areas of study that would yield, to them, a knowledge of those things to be discussed.

Shouting matches avail nothing.   There is an old adage that states that a man convinced against his will is of the same opinion still. This is, especially appropriate to this discussion.   One cannot overwhelm another with a preponderance of evidence or the strength of voice if the facts are not salient, appropriate and calmly presented. Even then, most often, the opponent will not admit that his stance was wrong and the best we can hope for is that he will, in his own time, review the facts presented in the context of this argument and will realize they have merit. He might then begin to adjust his thinking on the matter.

I find people in the legal professions to be the most difficult to deal with in this way. To them, lies are a way of life... they are the commonplace and the ordinary. If they have been in this field for any length of time, they are no longer capable of recognizing truth from a lie and will not even try. If an item goes against the logic of his position, he will simply reject it out of hand. When dealing with these people, and with others of their ilk, it is best to merely present one's case and close the argument.   Cite the references that pertain and leave no statement without reference. To do this will go far towards making a good presentation to these people. Do not undertake to argue them into submission. Believe me, they have heard every lie ever known to mankind and are experts in spouting them back.   Be very strict in requiring references for any allegations they should make. Finally, remember this, I have NEVER learned anything worth knowing from someone who agreed with me totally... I learn from hearing a different opinion and investigating the truth of it. Be prepared to learn when you are in discussion and never be afraid to do so liberally.

Chapter 3-2
The Day of Destiny

What followed in the nearly half century to follow this momentous day has been an epic in incredulity. Expert after expert has testified to the veracity of the many aspects of this film. They have been largely ignored in favor of the statements of people who have no idea of what took place that day so long ago. Many people have even come forth to say that they were the subject in the suit... even though most could not identify were Bluff Creek even was, let alone how it could have been done.

Understand, there is no controversy among the experts who examined the evidence first hand at the time of discovery. The controversy comes from the statements of people who have no idea of which they speak and have no credentials to support their claims. Those who know the least are often those who speak the loudest.

With this in mind, this section is dedicated to the testimony of qualified experts. All statements contained are cited by name and credential. Now, to the facts...

Muscle Bulge:

Very early on in the Patterson-Gimlin Film, at Frame 5, an

anomaly shows up on the right upper leg of the subject of the film.

Very evident in the frame, there is a bulge in the quadriceps muscle. This is not a gunshot wound as some have purported nor is it something someone would design into a suit being built for the purpose of a hoax.

Doctor Andrew Nelson of the Center for Motion Analysis and Biomechanics stated: "This is probably a rupture of the Quadriceps Muscle... this is something that cannot be copied in a suit."

He continued, "After analyzing the biomechanical issues, I find it very hard to believe somebody in 1967 could have fabricated the intricacies as evidenced by the soft tissue irregularities seen on the upper leg. The science at that time was just far too primitive."

John Chambers, now deceased, who won the Academy Award for costume design in 1969 for the 1968 award winning movie, "Planet of the Apes" stated: "If this is a suit, it is the finest ever devised for it was beyond our capability in the 1960s. Every hair would have had to have been individually attached to the model for this to do what it does in that film."

Figure 3-3 Creature Maker John Chambers

My question is very simple... Having heard what the experts in the field have said about this apparent rupture, does this sound like something that could have been accomplished in the remote wilds of northern California by two rodeo rough stock

66

riders with no costuming or theatrical experience on a suit made of the hide of a red horse, as suggested by one fake Patty?

Size and Gait:

Professor Jeff Meldrum, Paleontologist, Idaho State University, stated that in primates the normal ratio of foot size to height is 6.5... that the foot is herein generally 15.5% of the height of the individual. It should be remembered that this is a "rule of thumb" only. There will be individuals who will not conform to this standard. That said, it should be noted that the general rule will still apply.

When Patty strode across that Bluff Creek sandbar, she left a very nicely defined trackway. Her prints were vivid and distinct, allowing the principles to cast the impressions using plaster of Paris as a medium.

Several noted authorities were called in to verify, independently, the scene. The measured size of the track as independently corroborated by John Green, Newspaperman from British Columbia, Canada, Bob Titmus from Redding, California and Al Hodgson of Willow Creek, California, all of whom saw and measured the tracks independently was fourteen and one half inches.

If we use the foot length as measured by independent sources, and apply it to Dr. Meldrum's formula we get a nominal height of nearly eight feet as follows:

14.5" Track X 6.5 = 94" = 7'10" in Height

Bill Munns, Graphic Artist, Hollywood set designer and analyst took a different approach to achieve a projected height for Patty. He had the Lens and Camera data and knowing the focal length of the lens, the magnification factor of that lens and the distance from the camera to the subject, he could ascertain the height of the subject of the film.

There was some confusion, initially, over what lens on the triple lens camera was actually used, but computations quickly solved that anomaly and Mr. Munns was able to state quite confidently that the being in the film was between seven and a half feet and eight feet tall as calculated.

The third method used to determine height utilizes the scene projected in Frame Seventy-Two of the film. We know that the length of the foot shown is fourteen and one half inches from the measurement of the tracks. If we allow for the shoulder slump, the bowed head and the knee bend of the right leg, and the fact that the right foot is sunken into the soil a finite distance, we can approximate her height by merely comparing the length of the foot as shown in the frame. I used a pair of dividers to apply the length of the foot to her over all height and came up with a height of seven feet two inches plus or minus three inches, or a ratio of about six point one times the foot length. That is certainly within the range to be expected from Dr. Meldrum's formula.

In this exercise we have used three different and distinct measuring techniques from three different experts to arrive at the same general conclusion: the subject in the film stood between seven feet four inches and seven feet ten inches. In no case did this study yield a figure that could be construed as the height of a normal human being found in society in 1967.

Gait:

The next area of study this treatise on height leads us is to the unique gait exhibited by Patty in the film. In order to shed some light on this area of interest, we must borrow from the world of make believe again and marry that to the world of science. Reuben Steindorf, Senior Animator at "Vision Realm, Inc.", using a system known as "Inverse Kinematics and Motion Analysis" created a 3D model of the subject in the Patterson-Gimlin film. This model was then forwarded to Dr. Andrew Nelson of the Center for Motion Dynamics and Biomechanics who graphically inserted a skeleton into the model of the creature.

Dr. Nelson ran an entire spectrum of tests on the test subject and determined that Patty walked with a "Compliant Gait". We humans, on the other hand, use a very stiff legged gait in which we, essentially, pole vault over our leg and land with a very heavy heel strike. Motion Capture analysis shows that the Compliant Gait results in a very smooth, swinging stride with virtually no heel strike and very flat-footed placement of the foot on the down step.

Dr. Scott Lind and Emmy Award winning animator Joe Russo then attempted to train an athlete to walk with this same compliant gait and found that the human body was not capable of exactly duplicating this movement. They were unsuccessful in their attempts to train even an athlete to walk with this gait.

This failure caused these professional men to conclude that it was impossible for a human to exactly duplicate the walking motion of the being in the Patterson-Gimlin Film.

Costuming:

An effort was made to analyze the possibility of the use of a costume in this short film. To this end, Peter Brooke, Costume Designer for the "Jim Henson Creature Shop" and famed Hollywood Costumer, John Chambers whose efforts on the "Planet of the Apes" took four professional designers three months to create, performed this examination and a thorough analysis of the being in the Patterson-Gimlin Film.

These consummate professionals concluded that there are three notable features in the film that needed to be closely examined and on which the conclusion depended. These three factors are:

1. Arm Length
2. Firm Musculature beneath the surface
3. The Hair Adheres to the body beneath it

We shall examine each of these points individually as we continue in our quest for the real facts as pertains to this film. It seems that all who I have ever heard denouncing this as a person in a suit do not know the facts that these experts have presented in their analysis.

Peter Brooke after his examinations stated unequivocally, "Such Costumes did not exist in the 1960s." The fur adheres to the form and contours of the body. Today we make such suits of four way stretch fur fabrics but that did not exist until the 1980s. The era of that film did not have fur that could be form fitted."

John Chambers added to Mr. Brooke's conclusions, "It does stretch. I don't know how they could have done that in 1967. There are several individual muscle groups that are plainly visible on the creature in the film." There is even "tightening and slacking of the Achilles Tendon

Figure 3-4 Bill Munns - Graphic Artist

evident" as she walks.

Mr. Chambers continued, stating that the "Shoulder blade is clearly visible and moves during the walk and the look back."

I believe that if I stopped here and ventured no further there could be few who could argue successfully that this film could in any way be contrived or faked. All of the factors mentioned to this point are patently visible and are easily seen by even the most ardent of skeptics... whether those skeptics would admit to seeing these factors is entirely another question and for that reason, if no other, we will go on with our treatise.

Bill Munns, Graphic Artist and Designer most noted, probably, for his large sized artistic representation of the ancient hominid, Gigantopithecus blacki.

Mister Munns has completed a thorough analysis of the requirements of a person wearing a suit such as one shown in the Patterson-Gimlin film would have to be. He was also completed an involved diagnosis of that film. I would recommend that anyone interested in this subject read his book, "When Roger Met Patty", visit his website at www.themunnsreport.com and his series of Youtube videos at:

http://www.youtube.com/watch?feature=player_emb edded&v=cJZTLWUJh-w#!

This is the first of a series of videos he has created concerning this subject. A treatise on the comparative anatomical features of a female model and the image of Patty is shown clearly in the video at:

http://www.youtube.com/watch?v=V9WO8c38cRo&fe ature=relmfu

In this work, Bill Munns carefully illustrates the motions of the person doing the filming and the subject of the film as they move through the setting of the encounter. He carefully illustrates the relative positions of both entities during this time frame. Part Two illustrates the trackway and the individual tracks therein. Part Three is the most important for our purposes. In this segment, Mr. Munns analyzes the subject in the film, Patty, and compares that to an actual female subject.

In Bill Munns's characterization, he points out numerous anomalies. He illustrates with side by side comparisons the impossibility of creating any suit like that which would have necessarily have to have been used in making the Patterson-Gimlin Film. His comparisons illustrate many incompatibilities inherent with placing a human into the anatomy of the subject of the film. His statement is that the anatomical differences leave us "with an impossible costume to construct..."

Mr. Munns stated, "The subject in the film has anatomical proportions that are very odd to say the least. Conventional creative costume design and tricks or illusions for altering regular human proportions do not achieve the result easily or effectively. Now, there are many ignorant people who have no knowledge of designing or fabricating creature costumes (that) will try to tell you differently because, in their ignorance, they fail to understand the difference between what is theoretically possible and what factually practical to accomplish. The simple reality is that... the human female shown could not be dressed up in any fur costume and make a perfect functioning performance equal to the Patterson-Gimlin subject performance. The challenge of putting a human into a fur costume to fake the PGF is far more difficult and questionable than the hoax believers claim that it is."

In short, Mr. Munns stated that "You cannot alter where the knees or elbows bend. She has long upper leg and short lower leg."

72

Due to the structure of the creature in the film, "If you could find a suit to match all the criteria necessary (a suit other experts have testified was not possible in 1967), you could not find a human who could wear that suit."

Arm Length Vs. Leg Length

Dr. Jeff Meldrum, Paleontologist, Idaho State University has taught a ratio known as the Intermembral Index or IM. Basically, the IM is the ratio of the arm length to the leg length of a subject times one hundred (to remove the decimal). In Humans this IM ratio is 72.

Figure 3-5 BBC Comparison To Patty
Property of BFRO-used with permission

In 1998, the British Broadcasting Company, BBC, approved and financed a program for their network to "disprove" the Patterson Gimlin Film by creating a state of the art costume and putting a man inside to prove that it could be done without a real sasquatch having to have done it. It is true that this project was being done over thirty years after the original film came into being. This new film would be taking advantage of all the latest technology available, with no regard as to its availability in 1967. They theorized that the people who made us believe in Wookies and Ewoks, Apes that ruled planets and all such creations would surely debunk the claim that the suit used in that long ago film was impossible to duplicate in these conditions...This is that suit:

There are two major differences in the suit pictured on the right with the man inside and the picture of Patty that are readily evident. First, pay close attention to the head and shoulder positions in the turn to look back.

Patty's head sits very low on her shoulders. Her neck is very short so that when she turns, her chin goes into her shoulder, preventing it from rotating further to the rear. The result is that the shoulder has to be rotated back and out of the way for her to swivel her head far enough to effect the "look back" seen in frame 354 of the film (erroneously reported as frame 352 due to inaccuracies in counting the frames). In the right suited figure, this is not a problem as the head sits high atop the pedestal that is the neck and can swivel over the top of the shoulder as it is shown doing here. The difference is quite obvious. The second obvious anomaly is created by the difference in the length of the arms. In that same right suited figure the right arm is in approximately the same position as its swing ends above the hip. That individual's hand is above the level of his buttocks. Compare that to the length and position of Patty's arm and hand. Her arms end well below her buttocks, not above as in the right suited figure. Once again, as in all such endeavors, not only was the Patterson-Gimlin film not disproved, but, in essence, it served to offer very good evidence for the veracity of that film. Aside from the fact that the person in suit could not begin to duplicate the compliant gait of the actual Sasquatch, a mere glance shows a very glaring error. Please note the relative arm lengths in the two figures. The right suited fake has arms that, in relation to the size of its body are HUMAN in form. The black figure, Patty, from the film frame 354, has arms that are much longer in relationship to her body. In fact, BBC, after airing this show issued a disclaimer stating that the data contained therein did not refute the claims of the Patterson-Gimlin Film.

Intermembral Index

Dr. Meldrum describes the Intermembral Index as the ratio of the arm as measured from the shoulder to the wrist, to the leg, measured from the hip to the ankle times one hundred. The one hundred factor is simply to clear the decimal from the result. Mathematically, that is Arm Length divided by Leg Length times one hundred or:

$$AL / LL X 100$$

In primate species, all members have a distinct and specific IM. They break down as follows:

In a human, the IM is 72
In a chimpanzee, the IM is 108
In a gorilla, the IM is 122
In a sasquatch, the IM is 84

As can be readily seen here, the IM of human and sasquatch are remarkably similar but certainly not identical. It is this difference that can be used to make qualitative evaluations on reported sasquatch photographs and videos.

75

If we return to frame 72 of the Patterson-Gimlin Film again, the arm length and the leg length are readily apparent and can be easily measured. Also, the arm and the leg are at the same distance from the lens in the same plane so no distortion or foreshortening is introduced into the exercise. The previously discussed calculation using the formula provided by Dr. Meldrum yields an IM of this figure to be 84. That measurement and calculation places it firmly into the range expected from its species.

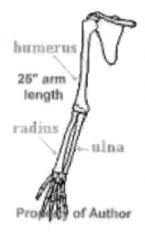

Figure 3-6 Arm Illustration

At this point the ardent skeptic, the sort that this treatise is designed for, would state something like, "Oh they just used an arm extender to make it correct..." Let us examine this more closely.

I measured my arm as best as I could in doing it alone and came up with the following data:

Arm Length = 25"...
Leg Length = 34.5"...
Therefore, my IM is:

$$25/34.5 \text{X} 100 = 72.4...$$

While this places me most firmly as human in structure, it creates a problem for he

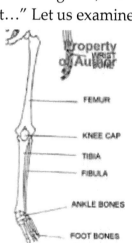

who would use an arm extender to achieve an IM of 84 as evidenced by the figure in the film. Solving the equation to yield a known IM is as follows:

Figure 3-7 Leg Illustration

$$(AL / 34.5) \text{ X } 100 = 84 \text{ or, } AL = 84 \text{ X } 34.5 / 100 = 29$$

This means, simply stated, that my arm length of twenty five inches

Figure 3-8 Arm Extender

would have to be extended by four inches to achieve the desired result. In viewing the figure here, where would that four inches be added? If it were done as in the figure above, that would make the lower arm well out of proportion to the upper arm. In Frame 72, it is very evident that the elbow is exactly where it should be placed in the arm. As has been stated prior: "The elbow cannot be relocated."

It simply is where it is.

A common ploy to trick the eye is to use oversized hands in the form of huge gloves to convey the idea of a longer arm. There was a recent video released by a fellow attempting to "disprove" the film... that film used this ploy, but the result was so emphatically terrible, it is beyond reason to ever believe it could be even remotely possible. Look at the hands in the film and it is readily apparent that they are in proportion to the rest of the body, not some out-sized grotesqueness perpetrated by one who would have us believe his tripe.

There is one other method for achieving the desired ratio. Perhaps one could reduce my leg length to the requisite twenty nine inches by somehow removing five and a half inches from its present length. Somehow, I think that might be even more objectionable to me than the process of adding the needed length to my arms. In short, there is really no feasible way short of surgery to alter this Intermembral Index formula or measuring criteria.

Know Your Players

Knowing your players is a very important concept in dealing with things pertaining to the veracity of any subject. It is especially pertinent here.

Do any of the skeptics denying the truth of this film know any of the persons they quote? Do they know that individual's propensity for truth vs. lies? Do they know what this person stands for in life? Have they had experience in business with them? What are the "fruits on their trees?" If they were accused in a court of law of being open-minded, would there be enough evidence to convict them? Do they know their players?

I KNOW Bob Gimlin personally and a nicer, more honest, more plainly humble gentleman has never existed.

Scott Sandsberry, a reporter for the Yakima (WA) Herald newspaper recently completed a sixpart series on the sasquatch people. In that series, he concluded with an assessment of Bob Gimlin's character. I would

like to share that here:

"Gimlin's version of what happened that day, though, has never changed. And he has had plenty of incentive to change it. Documentary filmmaker Doug Hajicek was working on a television show called 'Mysterious Encounters' more than a decade ago when, while talking to Bob Gimlin for one of the episodes, happened to (have) called the show's producers. When he mentioned he was sitting with Gimlin, Hajicek said, the producers told him to offer Gimlin $1 million to tell how he and Patterson faked the footage. 'It was instant. He didn't even have to think about it,' Hajicek said. 'I wasn't floored by it. I'd gotten to know Bob and he's just such a man of character. He doesn't lie.' He said, 'well, that's nice, and I'd like to take your money, but this is what happened: We came around this bend ...'"

That is Bob Gimlin. The man will look you straight in the eye when he tells you what happened that day. He does not equivocate; he does not stammer nor stutter. He tells you what happened and, as he told me, "There were three people in that crick bottom that day, Thom. There was Roger, there was me and there was that creature. There was no one else. There was nobody named Bob Heronimous." That's good enough for me because I KNOW Mr. Bob Gimlin!

Conclusions on the
Patterson-Gimlin

Figure 3-9 Bob Gimlin Portrait

Film:

Each of the experts cited in this section arrived at an independent conclusion and we shall look those now.

Analysis of the herniated quadriceps muscle by Dr. Andrew Nelson and John Chambers led them to conclude that the creature in the film is NOT a fake or a hoax.

Analysis of the size of the being in the film and the compliant gait of that subject by Professor Jeffrey Meldrum, Doctor Scott Lind, Designer and Creator Bill Munns, Designer Rueben Steindorf and Designer Joe Russo led them to conclude that the being in the film is of a height between 7'3" and 7'10" tall and that it walks with a gait that cannot be exactly duplicated by even an athlete.

Analysis of the costume itself by Peter Brooke, Bill Munns and John Chambers, all very well known in the costuming world and all award winners for their work, concluded that the materials needed to produce an effective costume of the type that would be necessary for that film were not available in the 1960s and even if they had been, no human could have physically been able to fill it and perform in it.

Applying Doctor Jeffrey Meldrum's Intermembral Index analysis to the figure in the film reveals an IM of 84, not the 72 found in humans nor the 108 or 122 found in chimpanzees and gorillas. 84 is the IM of Sasquatch.

It is VERY important to note here that if only ONE of the FOUR facts attested to her are true, then the figure in the film cannot be a man in a suit. That all four are attested to by qualified experts in their field yields extremely strong evidence of the veracity of the hypothesis that she is, indeed, *a REAL SASQUATCH and not a man in a fur suit.*

Chapter 3-3

The Massacre Theory Hoax

When our two men rode up that small creek bed in northern California they were searching for a myth... a creature who did not exist according to science. In the afternoon of that day, those men, mounted on their saddle horses and leading a pack horse rode around a large root wad left from one of the myriad trees washed out in the infamous 1964 floods that inundated most of northern California. With that small step, they rode out of obscurity and into destiny.

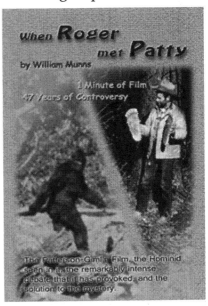

For nearly five decades now, science and the public has tried their very best to debunk those few frames of film that gave truth to what a lot of us had known to be the case for many years prior. It appears that every major attempt to discredit the subject only results in proving it further. There are many

Figure 3-10 "When Roger Met Patty" B. Munns

81

experts like John Chambers and Peter Brooke who have testified publicly that it would have been **IMPOSSIBLE** to make a suit to do all that was seen in that film in 1967... but, it seems that there are many who are simply not to be swayed by facts when their minds are made up. Today we are again assaulted by one such who tirelessly advances his pet theory, even though it makes absolutely no sense when viewed in the light.

Sometimes, with the slightest of provocation and the least of facts, people manufacture controversy. This film was certainly not apt to escape such treatment either. A television special was created using frames from the film. Of course, the special's producers did not have access to the first generation film, nor even a high level copy, but had to make do with a copy of a copy of a copy, as it were... in that effort, an artifact was introduced in one frame. In the tv film, Frame 613 introduced an insignificant light flare which, through the processes used in making tv copy, was introduced in a slighter from into the next frame. Some sharp eyed (if dimwitted) soul with a very lively imagination theorized that those were muzzle flashes from rifles being fired by persons unknown who were shooting at the sasquatch beings who were being filmed. If this theorist had exercised an ounce of ingenuity and had realized that a copy was being used, he would have checked a better source... i.e. a higher level copy and would have seen that the flare did not exist there. At the very least, if he had have checked with someone knowledgeable in the mechanics of film, he would have saved a great deal of trouble.

This is seldom the case however, and even though the entire theory falls apart when investigated coherently, this did little to dissuade neither the originator of this theory nor the adherents that perpetuated it. Even today, there are those that persist in perpetuating it.

Mr. Bill Munns treats the technical aspects of this phenomenon thoroughly in his excellent book, "When Roger Met Patty". I will leave the reader to his instruction for the nuts and bolts of this anomaly.

A few years ago, at a conference in Ohio, someone advanced the application of this theory that Roger Patterson and Bob Gimlin did not encounter one female sasquatch that October day, but many and their response was to immediately shoot and kill several of them. It was hypothesized that they obtained a backhoe to use in burying the bodies of these several dead beings. The evidence cited does not bear up under scrutiny to anyone who understands the situation there. Very few of those espousing this ludicrous theory have ever even been to the site, let alone investigated the claims.

The theory does not state how they happened on so many of these elusive creatures to begin with, nor does it offer any explanation as to why these intelligent beings, if so encountered would stand around allowing two men (only one of whom had a rifle as the other one was carrying a camera) to decimate their ranks with shot after shot, felling first one then another. I don't recall how many were allegedly murdered in this fashion. I've heard numbers that varied from five to nine. Bob was, indeed, armed with a 30'06 bolt action rifle. This rifle will hold five rounds in the magazine. Bob has stated to me that it was loaded with 180 grain bullets, his elk load... Perhaps those "other men" were doing the shooting?

Let us examine this precept a moment. In all accounts where men have purportedly had to shoot at these creatures, in no case was there ever a one shot kill. In the case of the Ape Canyon incident, many shots were fired and no bodies were ever found. It boggles my mind to think that Bob could then expect to kill five of these beings with five shots. The sasquatch weigh between five hundred and nine hundred pounds with some going larger than that. Let's compare that for a moment to an elk. I have hunted elk and I have taken many of them. A mature Roosevelt Elk will have a very similar body mass to the described sasquatch. I have NEVER had a one shot kill on a mature elk. Not ever... the minimum was two shots and I have taken as many as five shots to anchor a large animal. Now, we are asked to believe that not one, but at least five such occurrences materialized? Of course, he could have reloaded... and, in fact, he would have had to have reloaded to murder creatures six through nine.

Bob's rifle was a Remington bolt action... a model I myself owned many years ago. In fact, my brother owns that rifle to this day as far as I know... it is top fed, meaning replacement cartridges are loaded through an open bolt down into the magazine one at a time. This takes considerable time. Now, think about this... what are these beings doing while he is reloading? Evidently, according to the theory, they are lining themselves up, one behind the other so more than one could be killed with each shot. Lest one think this possible, I have never had that bullet from that rifle penetrate an elk completely. Never...

This begs another question... since we know that it was impossible for one person to have perpetrated this disaster, if Roger was indeed, helping with the murders... where did the film of Patty come from? Perhaps he filmed her before the massacre and the victims all stood around and watched while the one subject exited the scene in a timely manner. If this was not the case, perhaps Patty came back to get her frames of glory after the others were all dead? No? Oh... okay. Yes, I understand I'm being ludicrous here but no more ludicrous than the basic premise is to begin with.

I wondered what "evidence" led to this outrageous theory in

the beginning. In researching it, I found that one of the main observations was what appeared to be, on first look, a pool of standing water. The author of this theory had postulated that this is not water, but is, in fact, blood. Why? ...Because it appeared red in the film...

Excuse me, but what time of day was this film made? Oh? Afternoon... At the bottom of a canyon with the sun sliding down the western sky... Every photographer worth his ASA/DIN number knows that the later in the day one goes, the lower the angle of the sun, the more RED there is in the light... add to that, this was late October. In the fall there are many shrubs that grow in this region that have leaves which turn red when the chlorophyll retreats to the roots for storage over the cold season of winter. A couple of the more prominent of these species that are found in the Bluff Creek, California region are vine maple (Acer circinatum) and poison oak (Toxicodendron diversilobum). There are others, of course, but these are prevalent in the area.

Figure 3-11 Poison Oak (Toxicodendron diversilobum)

In addition, the trees growing on that flat creekbottom are RED Alder... Alnus rubra (rubra being Latin for RED...). Most of those trees pictured in the flat are broken and bleeding red alder, having been survivors of a hundred year flood only

85

just prior to this event. When red alder is damaged and the bark torn, it exudes a red tinted fluid...

Now, is it any great question where a red tint to that water might have come from? Is it still a mystery to anyone?

Another comment concerns the supposition that the hunters might have been using dogs to chase the sasquatch because what appears to be a dog track appears in one photo. This area is wild with coyotes... wild dogs... there are wolves known to roam here as well... another dog... and a week after the film was shot, dogs were, indeed brought in in an attempt to trail Patty... unsuccessfully, of course as I have never seen a dog who would track a sasquatch. They simply will not do it.

In 1967, there was very little logging occurring in the region due to the incredible storm. Roads were in a terrible state and simply could not yet sustain the truck traffic necessary to haul the logs. The washed out logs in the creeks had been salvaged, for the most part, but little logging was going on then. I worked for a major timber company some eleven years later and we did log in that drainage and little had been done before us.

Figure 3-12 Hi Lead Logging

For the final nail in the coffin of this foolishness, consider this... In 1967 there was no taboo against shooting one of these creatures. In fact, he was being actively hunted in many areas... always without success. Roger wanted a film to prove his thesis of their

86

existence, but what would have proven it better, or would have supplemented a film more than the body of a sasquatch? Then, as now, scientists would have clamored for such. Why in the world would anyone seeking to prove their existence in the absence of any form of censure not have brought one of those bodies out to, at least, have it mounted to display with his film? It totally defies any kind of logic that this could have been the case.

The Hoax, Part II

As is fairly common with such people as those who author these fantasies, as soon as this argument was logically presented, the scenario changed... it was no longer Bob and Roger who were the trigger men, but the "Evil Timber Companies" who were doing this to protect their interests. Of course, there was no evidence of this evil doing, just the rantings of an individual.

Do I believe it impossible that a timber company would do things to ensure the continued viability of their businesses? Oh yes! Without a doubt they would and have! I have, personally, known of incidences where timber companies have perpetrated hoaxes to help their cause. Most commonly, as in the case of a major timber holder on Washington's Olympic Peninsula, they created fake tracks... such as those faked by road builder Ray Wallace in 1958 in

Figure 3-13 Fake Footprint - Blue Creek

this same Bluff Creek area.

The tracks they are left were in an area where they are sure to be found and were ludicrously easy to identify as false. The rationale, was simple... if this set of tracks is found to be fake, that makes every track ever found in the history of man fake as well in the minds of the general public. With this history intact, now, whenever new evidence is found, they can simply laugh it off as another incident of fake tracks... "After all, weren't those found in our yard office parking lot proven to have been faked? It's just another case of the same thing!" Hence, there is less danger to their operations from the machinations of the preservationists that plague all those who would use the wild places.

What mitigates against this possibly being the case in this instance? What factors are different from the scenario just presented? To begin with, that company in Washington owned its own timberland... they were protecting access to their own resources. The land at question in California is publicly owned. It

Figure 3-14 Bluff Creek Drainage Showing Harvest Units
courtesy Tom Yamarone

is part of Six Rivers National Forest and is owned by the American people and managed by the U.S. Forest Service branch of the Department of Agriculture. There is no "evil timber company" involved in the process.

To explain that process... At that time in history, the Forest Service was charged with managing the timber resources within the National Forest system, including the sales of standing timber to feed the need for lumber and paper products in the world. Periodically, the USFS would determine how much timber could be removed from the National Forest in question and still maintain the charges the managers had to maintain a sustained yield and multiple uses of the forests.

The individual Ranger District, in this case, Orleans Ranger District of the 6 Rivers National Forest, would mark out the areas that would be their highest priorities for harvest. These "Sales" would then be advertised for bid.

There might be as many as thirty or more timber companies and sawmills bidding on any single sale depending of a myriad of factors including timber type and grade, distance to their manufacturing facility, ease of harvest and many others. All bids are sealed. There is no opportunity to change one's bid when bidding is declared closed... a time designated in the sale information.

The winning bidder then had a specific period of time to build needed roads to access the standing timber, log the sale units and transport the wood off the ground. This, being USFS wood, it was not eligible for export in raw log form. It had to be manufactured in some way domestically, usually into the form of lumber, plywood or wood chips for paper, depending on the grade of the particular log. It should be noted that the resultant product was then deemed qualified for export. Also, many companies that had their own timberland holdings could and did purchase these sales to run their domestic mills so they could export the timber off their own land to gain the higher prices paid for export logs than what could be realized for logs used for domestic production.

Once the buyer was determined through this bid process, he would then engage contractors to construct the necessary road, fell the timber, log the timber and haul the logs to his required destinations. Often, a prime contractor was engaged and all the subsequent legs of harvest would be effected by that entity. A single buying company might have as many as thirty or more contractors available to them that they used as occasion demanded. Likewise, a single contractor may work for multiple buyers, either simultaneously or separately.

It should be obvious from this description that the concept of an "evil timber baron" simple does not work.

Conclusions

In view of the actual evidence as presented here in a logical, respectful manner, I do not believe that anyone with more than four active brain cells could possibly have believed that this "theory" could possibly be true... and we did not even discuss where the mystery backhoe that would have been necessary to bury so many large bodies came from, how it got three and a half miles back up a narrow, steep sided creek channel to the film site in order to do this work and who would have operated it in this rocky defile... and, lastly, it's just this. Bob Gimlin looked me directly in the eye and said, "Thom, that day there were three beings in the bottom of that canyon... There was Roger, there was me and there was that creature... there was no one else nor was there anything else that happened other than what you see there and what I have related..." and I believe him because, above all else, Bob Gimlin is a genuine MAN... there is not an ounce of coyote in him and there is even less back up.... (One might have to be a cowboy to understand the last, if you have trouble with it, contact me and I'll explain it to you...)

It's most interesting to me that none of those promoting this poppycock will look me in the eye and speak straight concerning it... Now... you decide... Those are the facts... they are not suppositions nor are they pipe dreams...

Part 4

Modern Bluff Creek

Courtesy Sue Funkhouser

Chapter 4-1

Del Norte Encounter

In the spring of 1978 I worked for a timber company located on the California-Oregon border at Highway 101. My job required that I drive from the mill yard inland to our logging jobs west of Orleans, CA. To get there, I had to drive a huge circular route.

Leaving the yard, I drove south on US 101 for just over sixty miles through the coastal Redwood groves to the Bald Hills Road just north of Orick, CA. I followed the Bald Hills Road for about thirty-six miles to Weitchipec, CA and Highway 96 where I turned north for approximately fourteen miles. At Orleans, I turned back to the west and drove for about twenty five miles to our job sites. Since much of this was driven on gravel roads, the trip required four to five hours to

Figure 4-1 Hiking the G-O Road near Blue Cr.

complete, depending on the amount of traffic on the highway. I was required to make this trip an average of three times a week.

There existed at that time a road that ran directly from the small town of Gasquet, CA, up the south fork of the Smith River and past Doctor Rocks, crossed Blue Creek at its head and descended on into Orleans.

This direct route shortened my trip to about ninety minutes and was known as the Gasquet-Orleans Road, or more familiarly, the G-O Road. It was paved on both ends, but there was, in the middle, from east of Blue Creek to the west of Doctor Rocks a stretch that had never been constructed beyond a bulldozed trace through the timber. The U.S. Forest Service had plans to finish this road, but was being fought vigorously by the lunatic fringe preservationists who pretty much control California, it would seem. The final result being that, today, the road is still not completed. In fact, much of it has been declared "Wilderness" by the powers that be... it seems odd reconciling wilderness with a paved road running through it!

Much of this primitive section of the road was at sufficient elevation that winter snows drifted deep and kept the track closed until early summer, at least, under normal circumstances. This particular spring, the shortcut being so important to us, we hauled a D-7 Caterpillar as far in the west end of the road as we could before the snow stopped us.

There, we unloaded the Cat and let him clear snow across the ten miles or so until he broke out of it on the east end. We used a rubber tired road grader to clear what drifts were amassed on the paved section east of the primitive road. At the beginning of the pavement, we reloaded the Cat back onto its trailer and hauled it on to our road construction site.

With the G-O Road open to Four Wheel Drive vehicles, our crews could leave home two hours before time to be at work on

Monday morning, work their time, spend the week in Orleans at a logging camp we'd set up there and return home after work on Friday. If there were something sufficiently important to do at home, they could make the trip in midweek, though this was frowned on. On the week in question, I had meetings scheduled with the U.S. Forest Service Sale Administrator on Thursday to set where the roads into the next unit would be located. I then had a conference with our road construction boss set for Friday morning. I determined to drive over on Thursday, have my USFS meeting, spend the night at our camp in Orleans, meet the road boss on Friday and drive home Friday afternoon.

I was meeting with government workers on Thursday so I knew I could sleep in a bit longer as they would not leave their office in Orleans any sooner than 8:30 am.

Since I knew I would be staying over, the pack I always carried with me in my truck in case of emergency was especially plush that Thursday morning as I pulled out of the mill yard at seven am. The sun was well above the eastern rim when I reached the snow line on the G-O Road. That I was the only vehicle to cross this morning was evident in the icy slush that was on the road in various places.

I had traveled about a half mile from the point the snow began and was on a slight uphill grade traveling west to east. I spotted tracks in the snow. The tracks came from the north, dropped down into a shallow swale that opened onto the road in a very muddy stretch. They continued on south, up the slight bank on the south side

Figure 4-2 Trackway in the Snow

95

of the road and disappeared into the distance.

My first thought on seeing the tracks was that a bear, just out of his winter's sleep had been on a trip of exploration, probably for his morning meal. I am always interested in locating sizable critters, and especially since there were no cub tracks I could see, it would most likely be a lone boar, I stopped short of where the tracks crossed in the mud of the road to measure this bear. As I walked up to the tracks, my jaw dropped like a rock! There in the muddy slush was not the bear tracks I expected to see, but a very large, very human shaped foot print... not just one, but a whole series of them!

Figure 4-3 Courtesy of Tot

For several moments I just stared! Bare, humanoid foot prints that measured just over eighteen inches in length with a stride that I, at six feet, four inches could not begin to emulate. For me, a full stride, left and right is exactly five feet in length. I've measured it time and again in my capacity as a forester. The stride on this creature was well over eight feet in length! That was an awesome stride! My first inclination, after regaining mobility, was to follow them to see where they led, and, hopefully, what was making them.

I had but little time to devote to this. A multi-million dollar logging operation could not be left to falter because I wanted to chase a sasquatch. I did flag the spot well, so I could find it easily on my return trip. I knew I could be done by noon on Friday because I did not have to wait on the USFS and could meet the road boss on the job at six am.

Noon Friday found me in my little truck, climbing the last grade out of Blue Creek Canyon that led to the crossing… not that I was anxious or anything. When I reached my markers, I found a secluded spot without much snow where I could park my truck out of sight of the road. I knew the cutting crew, the logging crews and the road building crews would be passing through here tonight and, knowing that most knew my truck, I did not want them to know what I was about doing here.

When I was ready to travel, I set out on the, now, day old tracks with little hope of catching up with this particular creature, but I had to follow. Down the ridge we went in the snow. Within a half mile, we broke out of the timber onto a sunny, south-facing slope that was clear of snow except in the very shaded areas. Every few hundred yards there would be a patch of snow varying in size from a few feet across to some that probably covered more than an acre. Although it was not difficult tracking in the bare trail that varied from damp to muddy, these snow fields served to let me know I was still on the same individual.

Very late in the day, when I felt I had hiked about eight or nine miles from the G-O Road, hunger was beginning to rear its demanding head so I decided to look for a good campsite, enjoy my dinner and take a little time to explore my immediate area before dark spread its tentacles and drove me back into camp. The area I was in was populated with stands of magnificent old-growth Douglas Fir of huge proportions. Some of these were more than seven feet in diameter and it was obvious that they had survived many, many fires. Between the stands, especially on the south facing slopes, the scars of those fires were very evident.

When I dropped down onto a flat gravel bar adjacent to a

beautiful, clear running stream, I thought I had probably found my campsite and when I noticed that several of the huge old behemoths had their trunks burned out, leaving a warm, dry, cave-like den, I determined that I was at home for the night. This had everything I normally look for in a campsite, level ground, cover from possible lightning storms that the current increasing clouds could certainly deliver, and abundant fresh, clean water.

The only disconcerting thing about my campsite was a rather putrid smell that wafted through from time to time and, in searching the den burned from the tree trunk, there were a large number of long, black hairs lodged in the bark and wood. I

thought I had probably found a bear's winter den and, since they were out and doing now, they would not mind sharing quarters with me, since I was determined I would not be there when next they needed it for

Figure 4-4 Burned Hollow Tree

hibernation. This area, as I have described it here was the model for the second Sasquatch camp in my book, "Ghosts of Ruby Ridge".

The first thing I did after getting out from under my pack was to hike up the stream for a couple of hundred yards, checking closely for dead critters lying in the water.

The coming night was just beginning its tenure when I heard

from the timber the most god-awful, gut wrenching, piercing, high, ululating cry. It was absolutely stunning and bone chilling to hear. I had, at the time, absolutely no idea what could be singing that song and I wasn't really sure I wanted to know. I had heard descriptions of the call of the sasquatch, but, believe me, no description I had ever heard even began to prepare me for the reality of it. The first call went on, varying in pitch and modulation for what seemed like minutes, but which was probably between thirty and forty-five seconds. It then ended by fading away in volume to zero.

I was sitting by my fire, completely at attention, eyes and ears under full strain to learn more when it began again though not in the same place. Where the first call was to the south, this call was from the northwest. Again, the same high ululations, almost a warbling sound followed by a steady tone only to be varied again. This time I was able to be a bit more clinical about it as I was not quite so in awe of the sound in and of itself.

I timed this scream at twenty-five seconds when it again faded away. When the calls ceased, there was not a sound to be heard from any source save two. The bubbling of the small creek which was wholly unimpressed with the nocturnal display I had just witnessed was one sound. The other was the thumping of my heart in my chest. I judged the calls to be just up the ridge from my lair, not over two hundred yards away from me.

After these two calls, nothing more was forthcoming. I built my fire up slightly so that it afforded more light. When about two hours had elapsed with no more contact, I noticed a shadow flicker across one of the openings to my den. A moment later, another shadow flickered like the first had. They were not really close to my tree, but just at the edge of the light cast by my fire. I quickly searched my pack for the flashlight I always carry there.

Unfortunately, when I found it, I could not get it to work. My pack seldom leaves my truck so that I always have it in an emergency. Normally, I remove the batteries from the hand light and store them separately in a plastic baggie to prevent what I had just discovered. Evidently, at some prior time, I had broken my own rule.

Without artificial light, I was relegated to making the most of the light my little fire afforded. By sitting near the opening with my fire at my back, I was able to see my "guests". There were three of them that I watched most of the night. Evidently, I had unwittingly commandeered their den and they did not appear overly pleased with the prospect of sharing it with me. At any rate, they were with me all night long, a night that lasted, I might add, approximately one hundred and seventy seven hours.

During those one hundred-seventy-seven hours, I was fascinated by what was happening. There were times when the large male would look directly at me and move his mouth, uttering a chattering like sound. I felt then and even more so today that he was doing all he could do to communicate with me although what he was saying was impossible for me to discern.

During this period, the female more or less remained in the background but watched events very closely. She did not appear to be upset or nervous, just interested. Even when her son approached my lair, she did not exhibit any undue stress or exhibit any aggressive tendencies. She did "speak" to him on occasion and he'd retreat a few steps from me... only to ease back toward me when he thought he could. He would sneak in at times and rap the tree with a stick, sending a resounding thump echoing in the timber.

My wish is that this incident could be done today... after I have learned so much more about them. I would have made more of an effort to communicate... probably not verbally, but perhaps, mentally or, more likely, with glyphs in the soil.

Towards morning, I dozed in short catnaps that were often interrupted by the sounds of woofs and yips that I heard from outside my nest! Somewhere near dawn, these sounds stopped and, my fire built up to last a bit more, I slept soundly for a time. When I woke, light covered the land, my fire was burned down to coals and the only sounds to be heard were those common to the mountains in the daylight hours.

On emerging from my retreat, the first thing I saw were myriad tracks. From these tracks, I discerned that there where, indeed, three separate creatures of three separate size classes. My assumption is that it was a family group; however, that is strictly an assumption on my part. One thing was certain though, the biggest fellow was the same one as I followed into this deep canyon. As soon as I had completed my breakfast and morning ablutions, I hoisted my pack and my butt and hied out of there and back to the road and my waiting truck.

This incident is factual and is reported here exactly as it occurred. The memory has remained bright in my mind though more than thirty five years have elapsed since that night.

Chapter 4-2

Elk Meadow Ronnyvoo

I had never had the opportunity to return to the spot of that fabulous encounter. I always expected to do so "next week" or "next month for sure" but before that could happen, I left that job and returned to the Pacific Northwest. Since this spot is nearly forty miles off a highway, it's not somewhere one trips over by accident. It has to be a destination... and a destination that is accessible for only a very few months a year. Because of that, my return just never happened... until June of 2014...

The Facebook Group, "Bigfoot Community" was planning an outing to Willow Creek in the wild area of northern California. I had no desire to "camp" in downtown so I devised a plan to establish a spike camp in the mountains, remote from their base camp. The idea was that any of those in the base camp would be welcome in our spike camp at any time.

When we started on the process to locate a suitable location, it was recommended we return to the Blue Creek area where the aforementioned incident occurred... as we worked further on the concept, this location just seemed to solidify in our minds. One group planned a hike into the canyon where the incident occurred, as closely as I could locate it, anyway! Others just wanted to be part of the high country gathering so, it happened... The Elk Meadows Ronnyvoo was born in our minds.

Exclusive of the group in town, we had Arla, Barb, Cathy and Wendy from the midwest in our camp plus Nancy and Russ from northern California... There was Sue and Kathi from Oregon, Jackie all the way here from England and there was me. We were the core group... the cadre upon whom all else was predicated. Others would come and go and some of us would stay here longer than others and a few would even move to lower elevations to escape the frigidly cold air prevalent at our altitude. But... this was our home for twelve days in June... this site... Elk Meadows... was the site of the crossing of Blue Creek as related earlier in the narration. I had returned to that point I had dreamed of since May of 1978.

Figure 4-6 Elk Meadows

There was a lot of space in this flat which meant we could spread out across a wide area. There was no one else camped within range of us... we did see a few people in the twelve days we were there, but no other campers joined us. There were a couple of parties of hikers who passed through at two different times and one party drove into our camp only to leave again quickly. All in all, we were essentially alone in this beautiful spot in God's creation. When camp was set up,

Nancy and Russ were at the north end and Jackie and I set up at the south end, approximately two hundred yards distant. The midwest ladies were about a third of the way from the north camp and Sue between them and my tent. Across the roadway, Kathi elected to set up away from others as she liked the interactions she got at night from those beings visiting.

Our cook fire and general camp area was just south of my tent about thirty yards distant. This area was surrounded on the south by large Port Orford Cedar trees with the beginnings of Blue Creek on the east, the road into our area to the west and the north opening to the meadow that was our home. Spanning the creek next to our fire pit were two large fir trees that had been upended in times recently past.

During our time at this beautiful spot, the encounters were nearly non-stop. Nightly we had large visitors in and around our camp. They left their tracks, they moved our gear and they watched us every day. Our time in the higher mountains was absolutely fabulous. Following are chronicles of some of the more noteworthy events of the time there...

Chapter 4-3
Wednesday 6-17-2014
1845

Close Encounter of the Hairiest Kind

It was hot in Willow Creek and the three of us who had made the sixty-seven mile, two hour trek into town were regretting our decision even before we left the Bigfoot Community (B.C.) camp at Camp Kimchee in downtown Willow Creek. We had discharged our duty to those camped therein... after we found  them... even though the B.C. Contingent were off on a field day trip to the Redwoods and the Pacific coast just a few miles to the west. We had completed our shopping but I passed up gasing up as the gas at the tiny reservation town of Weitchepec was seven cents cheaper than here in town... or, it was until we got back to it to find they'd raised their prices for the upcoming weekend as well...

Figure 4-7 Orleans, CA

We filled our propane tank as well since this was the first time we'd used the tent heater on high and, believe me, running out of gas for your heater was not to be contemplated at our high elevation camp where ice routinely formed on the outside of the tent before morning! All things accomplished, we pointed our collective nose homeward on the G-O Road from the Orleans (O) end...

As we climbed the grade that led us from town, all of us were awake and alert... we had seen deer and bear on this road virtually every time we had traversed it and certainly did not want to miss the opportunity to do so again. At least, that is what I told myself and that it had nothing to do with the fact that I was working very diligently to reduce the two hour drive time to less than ninety minutes... We had seen bear ranging in age and size from newly emancipated two-year-old twins to a huge old boar that is probably as large as any bear I have ever seen in the lower forty-eight. This old boy did not wait around for a portrait nor even for introductions but we had seen him clearly, in the middle of the road in bright sunlight at a range of less than thirty yards. He was large enough of head and body that his ears appeared tiny in comparison... an important clue in judging the size of any bear. I estimated his weight to be in excess of three-hundred-fifty pounds and probably closer to three-hundred-seventy-five pounds but not over four-hundred pounds. For northern California, he was certainly a very large bruin!

This fellow matched the description, size and and color both, of a big fellow spotted earlier by Arla, Barb, Cathy and Wendy, the crew from Oklahoma on their trip into the camp area. Although certainly a black bear, Ursus americana, and not a grizzly, Ursus horriblis, it was of a grayish brown coloration and not the shimmering black displayed by so many of those found here. It should be noted here also that of the twin two-year-old bears spotted, one was the typical satin black and the other this same

106

unusual brown shade. This caused me to reason that this huge old boar was probably the sire of these twins and was most probably the dominant male in this region... the bull of the woods, so to speak!

Having all this experience so fresh in our minds, we were especially alert to our environment and hoping so to repeat our encounters. Our little troupe had not yet passed the Six Mile post on the GO Road when I rounded a curve, one of approximately two-hundred-sixty-eight thousand of them on the final thirty miles of our trek... and there standing directly in the middle of the road, again in bright sunlight, was another pure black phase bear. He was, I believe, another two-year-old not long from his mother's protection. He also did not wait around for introductions nor other civilities, but in a matter of five or so paces, swept into the brush that lined the road in such profusion at this point... within but moments he was gone in the physical form as his after image was fading from our eyes.

Figure 4-8 G-O Road

On we traveled with me pushing as hard as the ubiquitous curves and deteriorating road conditions would allow... perhaps even faster a time or two! Actually, I had cut my driving teeth on roads such as this one... I had literally learned to drive a car on roads in far worse condition than the GO Road, even in the state of disrepair they had allowed to happen here. It was, at least, paved

107

and, with the exception of those areas where the roadway was slumped due to poor design and poorer maintenance, could be traveled at speeds of over forty-five miles per hour. To maintain this speed did require nearly constant braking and hard acceleration coming out of curves. I must admit though, I was really enjoying it as it is so seldom we are allowed to actually drive any more. Even when we get on a road that presents the conditions that would enable it, speed limits, traffic and police officers minimize the actual enjoyment, if not the opportunity itself. Such was not the case on this road today. I am not sure if my passengers were in total accord with my joy or not, but for the most part they were quiet and seemed to enjoy the ever-changing view. A time or two, I even caught one or the other with their eyes closed, though in repose or in prayer, I never knew for sure... I must admit I was a bit nonplussed on Saturday as we were crossing over Grayback Mountain between Cave Junction, Oregon and Happy Camp, California and Jackie asked me for a pen and paper so she could write out her name and vitals with the name and contact information of her next of kin which she then put into my glove box! Since this had occurred some days prior and not today, I didn't look at it as anything to be concerned over and continued on my way at my pace on our return to our home camp.

Just past Mile Post Fourteen it happened... and we witnessed a most interesting event. As I have described, there were three of us in my car. I was driving, Jackie, having come here for the Ronnyvoo from far-off Devon, England was riding shotgun in the front passenger's seat with Arla directly behind her in the REO position. At the time of this event, Arla had her eyes closed and witnessed only the aftermath. Jackie was alert and I was extremely alert, given the driving I was doing.

At a fairly good rate of speed, we rounded a curve and transitioned from sunlight to full shade. It was nearly seven pm so the sun was at a low angle in the sky and our west to west-northwest route had been giving me fits with the sun in my eyes, making the transition to shade most welcome!

As soon as the transition was complete and my eyes adjusted to the new light level, I saw two figures standing directly before my car and a bit over half way to the right hand side of the two-lane roadway when viewed from my vantage point. This placed them well into the right quadrant of the roadway. The two individuals immediately turned and, with but two paces, crossed the roadway back to my left and exited it on my left side.

My initial thought was "BEAR", but that was immediately dismissed as they were both erect and moving bi-pedally. My next thought was "MAN"! That died aborning as these were much too large to be men. I was looking UP at them from the seat of my car at a range of less than twenty yards and more probably at a range that would not exceed ten to fifteen yards. It should be understood that these thought shifts were immediate! There was no consideration nor deliberation involved. My mind merely cycled through these options, discarding the inappropriate and storing a living image of the conclusion reached. The entire cycling, I'm sure, did not last a full second in real time.

Instantly, I knew what I was seeing! There were large – very large... exceeding seven and a half feet and probably attaining more than eight feet in height. They were entirely hirsute, except for their faces which were remarkably bare, and their feet, they were completely covered dark, steel gray and black pelage. Their shoulders were humped as they moved rapidly and their Ostman Pads shone brightly as they made haste to flee from our sight. It was the work of but moments for them to cover the width of that road with the second step taking them over the side of a bank that exceeded one-hundred-forty percent slope. In the blink of an eye they were gone but for that instant their image burned a scene onto the retina of my eye. That image has not dimmed with time, but is as bright as it was that day.

For just a few seconds we sat and reflected on what we had seen... the sound of Jackie's exclamation of "Bigfoot" was still ringing in my ears when a most amazing sequence of events was set into motion. Jackie, from her shotgun position, saw them as quickly as I did... She recognized them immediately for what they were... Then she started recanting. I could see her mind working to convince herself that she had not seen what her brain knew it had seen and what was real.

"No," she said, "not bigfoot but men with rucksacks on... "

"They were men... I could see their shoes they were wearing... they were dressed alike in gray wool shirts and pants..."

This continued all the way back to our camp where upon she had totally convinced herself

Figure 4-9 Turtle Rock

she had seen nothing more than two men in rucksacks, identical gray wool shirts, pants and like colored flip flop shoes cross a double lane road in a step and a half and dive down a one-hundred-forty percent side slope to escape view... Why any of this would have been necessary remains unexplained...

Chapter 4-4
6-20-2014
1030

Kathi's Story

The last tendrils of flame had diminished into the depth of the night at our campfire. It had been a very full day with a four hour round trip to Willow Creek included.

While in town we had enjoyed a restaurant cooked lunch, an outing to Al Hodgson's "Bigfoot Museum" where I was invited to show my three books now

in publication and asked to consider

Fig 4-10 Willow Creek Museum

speaking at their annual festival. There was also a visit to the Bigfoot Community Camp to meet and interact with those who had trekked there for that purpose... the one hour and forty five minute drive back to camp was pleasant but without incident, a rare occurrence during this twelve day outing, as we saw only the small critters of the biome and none of the megafauna who reside there. It was the first time in a week that we had made the circuit without seeing at least a bear. There were ample deer, quail and grouse in evidence to assure us that all was well, herein, however.

The evening drive was most pleasant with the day's light below the western ridges except for the occasional and rare moment we could surprise Grandfather Sun in his daily task of making the mundane of evening into the spectacular of Sunset. Tonight he seemed to be especially diligent in providing a Premium Quality experience. It became such that there was absolutely nothing to do but stop and record some of his better works. We had just made the transition from the paved surface of the 15 Road onto the rough and rocky 14NO3 Road when his full majesty manifested itself as Chimney Rock with his partner Turtle Rock emblazoned themselves across the canvas of his sky. We three travelers were simply in awe of the view as shutter after shutter snapped in recording the scene.

Two and a half miles and some fifteen minutes later, our little troupe spotted smoke rising from the area of our camp's fire ring. We knew we had brought our fire to its "Full Out" condition before leaving for town this morning so I suspected what was happening and, surely enough, as we passed Stanley (our trustworthy portapotty chair...) and his guarding minions to have a full and unobstructed view, there was our Nancy busily getting our fire built up against our imminent return. The timing was impeccable as we were able to exit our car in the rapidly diminishing rays of light to the warmth and comfort of a welcome home fire!

Dinner was done, the dishes clean and stored when the evening's "entertainment" commenced. In addition to the usual litany of stick snapping, tree knocking and grunts, our hairy hosts added a repertoire of howls to the night air. Although not close, these long, even howls were just up the ridge from us. Indeed, they were near enough that no nuance of sound was lost to us. That we had visitors in the creek immediately behind our camp was evident. The sounds of walking in the creek bed and the movement and chucking of rocks was apparent.

By this evening, number seven in camp, we were nearly immune to the foibles and follies of the indigenous hairy people. Jackie had retired and Kathi and I remained by the fire a while longer in hopes of more intimate contact. Finally, the long day began to exact its revenge on us... especially me... so I bid her a good evening and retired to my tent and my ritual of preparing my evening medications, my bed and my reading material.

It was the work of several minutes to accomplish all necessary to allow me to retire. My medications were taken, Insulin injections complete, clock wound (I hate awaking in the dark of night and wondering just what the time was...), heater lighted and clothes and paraphernalia arranged and stored against the night. Since, on this night, there were to be but two of us in my large tent, this storage was a bit more haphazard than is normally the case.

There were two items that caused me to smile when I arranged my tent for sleeping. First was the beautiful Father's Day card I received from my newest friends, Nancy and Russ "Gizmo" Cobb (I have never seen ANYONE so adept at making something utile and desirable from next to nothing in my LIFE!). The other is a stone... just a piece of igneous rock with an inordinately high iron content that called to me as I moved through camp early on in our stay. It should be noted here that stones and I have long felt an affinity for one another to the point that, when younger... in the middle years of the last century... it was not uncommon for me, after a particularly exceptional day of feeling "called" by one stone or another, for my jacket pockets to arrive back at my home a full

113

ten to fifteen minutes after I did! Now that said, I smiled as I moved this "special" stone to its night resting position from its daytime post.

My nest had been built and I was just undressed but not yet in my bed when it came out of the night... it was loud... as loud as any utterance I had heard this trip, causing me to immediately climb back onto my feet...

"THOM... THOM..." the cry resounded off the surrounding cedars... "Help me Thom... I can't move... Oh my brother... my sister... I'm so sorry but you scared me! I didn't expect you to be there... THOM! I need help now! Oh, my dear brother or sister, I'm so sorry... Thom, where are you?"

"I'm coming Kathi," I called out to her... "Just let me get my pants on and I will be there in a moment..."

"Hurry... I can't move and he's HUGE... Please hurry!"

Fig 4-11 Kathi's Tent

For all those who know me, it's understood that my "hurry" mode is not all that fast with the exigencies of age plying their wares on my physicality, but I really did do my best to speed my way along... even to the point that I disregarded the need for such amenities as shoes, socks or jacket in my desire to rescue this damsel from her durance vile.

It must be understood that, until now, I had no idea of what this threat was constituted. I knew not what the plague consisted of nor did I know how close disaster actually was. My first thought was "bear" as we had been seeing so many of them in our travels. Nancy had even had an encounter just up the road from camp no more than a hundred and fifty yards from Kathi's obviously now beleaguered tent. Her appealing to it as "brother or sister" tended to make me disbelieve this bear theory, as I knew of no such beings in her close family, former spouse notwithstanding.

Kathi is not one to panic at shadows on the wind. She has had encounters with the sasquatch people before and had met them logically and forthrightly. If she was now exorcised, there was reason, so I kept up a constant conversation, albeit one way, with her as I made my way to her side. I'm not sure she ever heard me as she continued her own stream of apologies to whatever was causing her distress and not paying me a whole lot of attention. Presently, I arrived at her side... not more than fifteen feet from her tent and possibly as close as twelve feet. As I watched her while approaching rapidly (for me...) I raised my eyes to follow the direction of her gaze... and saw...

"Oh my gosh," I uttered in a barely audible tone... Then, more loudly, "Well, hello, Big Guy... How are you tonight?"

As Kathi had left the fire pit after having disassembled the fire and walked the few yards to her tent, she was well at peace within herself. As she passed the few small trees that grew beside the road at the edge of the green meadow where her small tent was installed she flashed her light in the direction of her tent and audibly though quietly said, "There's my tent..." as the light flashed across the reflective material on the front of the nylon. There was no response of any kind, nor was any such required or expected. When she had taken but a very few more steps toward the structure, she again raised her hand light to illuminate it more fully.

What occurred then was most remarkable. As the light shone forward, a large, dark body reared up from just before the shelter. They were eyeball to eyeball at not more than ten feet separation. From my position inside my tent in the pursuit of making up my bed, I heard his grunt but did not, at that time, register it as anything more than one more greeting in a plethora of such I had so far absorbed this week.

The large fellow rose to his full height... probably as alarmed by the encounter as was Kathi. Our girl, however, could not raise her light at all. She was locked on to his waist area and could neither elevate her light nor her eyes any higher. As such, she had a very good and solid view of him from the waist down only. She had seen his torso as he stood, but could no longer focus on it.

Kathi was frozen in place. She could move no part of her body whatsoever. When I arrived at her side and greeted him, she was locked in her stance. Her head was low and her eyes cast downward. Had I not have greeted him verbally, she would not have known I had moved up behind her.

...But I had... and what I saw in my light, dim though it was, was a large, very male sasquatch standing beside a twenty foot, or so, tall cedar tree watching us intently. Kathi continued her exhortations, apologizing profusely and sincerely for having startled

Fig 4-12 Kathi

him. At the same time, he was attempting to apologize to her and the ensuing non-communicative conversation was quite amusing to me when seen from the outside.

Eventually, she calmed as did the big fellow and by taking her arm and telling him that I would assume responsibility for her, he released his lock on her and I instructed her to get her kak from the tent and move it into mine for the night. It is important to understand that this physical lock he used is a positive thing. If she

116

were allowed to run at will, she might well have fallen and injured herself badly. Perhaps she would have panicked and run directly at him or into the path of others in the vicinity. By locking her up, he was able to render her safely unable to move and to make his exit without further harm or trauma.

Although the clan remained with us all night long, poking and prodding our tent at times, no further incidents of this magnitude occurred and before morning, Kathi was up and doing and even had the fire going and coffee on before I arose!

Chapter 4-5
6-22-2014
0815

Camp Life

The sun had not yet made its appearance, although the fire was warm and bright. Daylight promised the advent of yet another gorgeous day.

I looked out from my tent where I was making preparations for today's departure to see Kathi... or, at least a reasonable facsimile of an early-morning version of a Kathi... I reflected a moment on how fortunate I was to have such a friend... Indeed, the three who attended this camp are of a sort that any person would marvel at their presence. Strong... Resilient... and Intelligent.

I had just left the fireside noticing the paucity of available firewood in the pile. It warmed my heart to see this woman, fresh from her night's rest, with her arms totally laden with wood... sufficient to last us, probably, for the few hours left to us here.

Since Sue and Arla had left camp, Kathi had stepped forward to assume the booshway duties while others had contented themselves with sitting on their collective butt and allow this to happen. Dinner last night had been left entirely to her devices though all were quickly in line when the call came that it was ready.

It was Kathi who cleaned up after... and even offered to make coffee for all...

I listened as Kathi approached the fire and asked those recumbent... "Have you brought in firewood yet?"

"Well, no," was the response. "I've only just gotten up."

"Yes, so have I, but to have a fire we need firewood and the standing rule is, 'if you come to the fire, bring wood.'" Kathi then deposited her load on the depleted stack and sat to enjoy the fruits of her labor while no one moved. Bugs returned to the fire from his morning chores with an arm load of wood... none other came in.

Breakfast came and went. Our guests from the low country were obviously enjoying the manifestations of our hosts. This morning alone, a new rock stack had been discovered as well as some glyphs and there was ongoing "conversation" with our big guys.

Deb had regaled us with her description of the vocalizations she had heard that sent her back to camp poste haste! Bugs and D'Anne had stayed out longer and had listened to even more of the back country talk but, eventually, even they had returned to camp filled with the excitement of the day.

Fig 4-14 Deb & D'Anne (r.) Discussing Events

While awaiting the return of our wanderers, a small party of hikers consisting of four men and two dogs, one with his own pack, passed by camp on the road that would lead them down the mountain. A moment's conversation told me they had hiked in over the divide from Dalton Creek. They returned mere moments later, retracing their steps to pass us again, this time in the direction of the end of the road. I assumed they were seeking the trailhead that would lead them on into Blue Creek Wilderness... an assumption that bore fruit moments later when I saw them headed in the direction of that trail and from which they did not return.

Upon the return to the fire of all three guests, Deb began to describe the discovery of this rock stack that was left in the vicinity... indeed, within feet of the small structure Arla had left a few days prior. It was at this point that obstructionism reared its head. "Oh, those hikers went that way – they made it."

I rolled my eyes and counted to ten slowly in order to stifle the retort that built within me. Instead, after a moment's calm, I said, "No, that is not possible. They were gone from us only long enough to have walked a hundred yards or so up that road... this shrine at the grotto is quite a distance beyond that."

The reply was, "Oh, they had to come in that way, didn't they? They must have made it then..."

I immediately and quietly rejoined, "No they did not come in that way... they hiked in from Dalton Creek Wilderness. If they had come in the road, it would have had to be at night as I have not left the vicinity of this fire since we returned from the Bigfoot Community camp on Friday evening."

While Deb was talking with me concerning the events she had been enjoying, she arose from her seat and walked toward the creek with the small bouquet of wild flowers she had picked prior. Her intent was to lay them on a downed log that spanned the creek. With a slight exclamation and in her very best Aussie accent, she said, "Look here... what is this," as she pointed to a tiny toy car that

120

had been left there. Deb continued on to describe how she had been searching thrift shops since her arrival in the United States for just such items as her husband at home collected them and she

Fig 4-15 Toy Car

wanted to find one for him as they were not readily available in Australia. This tiny replica of a 1955 Ford Thunderbird, complete down to the portholes in the hard top was obviously old. The wheels and axles were missing and it had been left behind some time in the distant past to be found by our hosts and deposited there as a gift to our resident from "down under".

Again, obstructionism reared its head when I heard, "Oh, some child must have been playing with it and left it there..."

I looked around at this person and just shook my head a bit... we had been camped in that spot, by this time, for over twelve days... twelve days during which <u>NO</u> child had been nearer than ten miles to that spot and probably not less than thirty miles!

I had a picture of that same log taken only days earlier that showed no toy car on it. Arla had walked across that log and there was no toy car on it! Yet today, there it was... We finally decided that, after querying all in camp, it had appeared on Saturday evening and Deb found it Sunday morning.

As we were marveling over this find and reflecting in the joy of the discovery and all it meant, I looked up to the second log that paralleled that on which the tiny car rested, also down and spanning the small stream to see a piece of well weathered grayed and worm holed driftwood perched precariously thereon. Once again, our skeptic stated, "That had to have fallen from the trees above..."

Fig 4-16 Wood Gift Left for Us

This time, I'm afraid I went a shade out of respect and replied, rather sharply, I regret to say, "Driftwood does not fall from trees! That piece of wood was placed there by a hand! It got there no other way!"

Even if the slab had been of the same type consistent with the surrounding trees, predominately Port Orford Cedar, and green or, at least, round in limb form, I would have serious doubts as to how it could have fallen vertically and lodged in that precarious position. This slab of driftwood was not in this spot on the day prior, Saturday, as Bugs had walked the log that day. Further, these two downed logs are immediately adjacent to our cooking area. The ice chest rests in the shade of the log holding the car and access between the two is used regularly by those descending to the creek for water!

I find it very humorous that in our discussions of their gifting, on multiple occasions, Kathi had asked for firewood as a gift. I'm not sure, no one could be, but is it possible this is Kathi's gift from them of fuel for our fire?

I find skepticism to be a healthy thing in dealing with interpreting the antics of these people, but when it becomes obstructionism, and ALL things are attributed to some oddball chance, that is beyond being skeptical... far beyond being of an open mind and is counterproductive. Question everything, but be willing to accept "I don't know" as a possible answer. Not all things are quantifiable... indeed, with these people, most are not... but all things are qualifiable! Cling to that for now until we can learn more.

Chapter 4-6

June 21-22, 2014

Bugs Mitchell's Account of Events

What follows is, in his own words, an account of the events occurring during the stay at Elk Meadows Spike Camp of Bugs, D'Anne and our Aussie friend, Deb who had obviously traveled the farthermost to attend this event. Deb was a total delight to her "'Murican" friends and she is welcome at my fire any time! In this case, the three had traveled from the BC Group's campground in Willow Creek to join us in the Meadows for a couple of days. I felt it important that this include the account of their stay as seen from their own eyes. This is that narrative:

This summer my friends Deb and D'Anne and myself attended the first annual Bigfoot Community campout in Willow Creek, California. While there we had the opportunity to go camping for twenty four hours in a remote part of the Northern California forest in a clearing known as Elk Meadow. It's located sixty-seven miles north of Willow Creek off of highway 96.

We left for the remote camp shortly before noon in Dee's

jeep. We had packed just enough stuff to stay for one night knowing we could sleep in a group tent. We had a relatively uneventful drive with no wildlife sightings or any other sightings

Fig 4-17 D'Anne and Deb on the GO Road

to report. We arrived around 1:30 pm to the camp and greeted friends Thom, Jackie, and Kathi. The location was absolutely gorgeous. It was a peaceful clearing with meadows and a creek surrounded by beautiful trees. There was a ridge to the north and a seven thousand foot peak called Turtle Rock to the west.

Shortly after getting acquainted with our surroundings in the meadow, I let the others know I was going for a solo walk north of the camp to see how far the road and paths led. The road ended at an empty campsite. I proceeded about three hundred or four hundred yards beyond this and stood on a large fallen tree. I stood there for a while being as still as I could and trying to be at peace with the beauty of it all. I was also a little tense and tried to keep my imagination in check. We knew there were bears in the area and I certainly didn't want to surprise one of them and I had come to experience bigfoot. One can get the picture. Just then I heard a wood knock to my right. It was clear... so much so that it startled me for a split second then silence. I waited motionless for about three to five minutes. I decided to take a few steps down the log and no sooner than I did another knock rang out at me as plain as could be.

Wow! This knock was definitely not a woodpecker as I had been hearing those since I arrived. No, these knocks were more substantial and singular, unlike the repetitive knocking from the birds. I waited another ten minutes but nothing else happened so I headed back to camp.

When I got back Thom informed me that Jackie, Dee, and Deb had gone south for a walk along the road. I met them as they were heading back toward me. They had just experienced some very strange noises and were a little spooked.

In an attempt to adequately describe these noises we called them a "gump" sound. We called it that because to us it sounded like a cross between a deep gulp and a very low frequency thump that could be felt in the chest. So we figured a gulping thump should be called a gump.

Deb, Dee, and Jackie explained that they had been walking along the road and started coming up to a section of the forest that had been burned. Deb started feeling very uneasy about the location and verbally expressed that to Dee and Jackie. Soon after that they heard the gumping sound directed at them. Jackie turned to them and asked what the heck it was and that it was reminiscent of sounds gorillas make. Apparently it took them quite by surprise and seemed quite out of place. Jackie did some howls and a few tree knocks but they didn't hear anything but the same gumps coming their way.

That night as we sat around the campfire, I whooped. We

wood knocked. Mostly, it was a very, very quiet night. But later that night we heard one very large tree break from the southwest. We also heard a "coo" and a "whoop". These were very delicate and came from what seemed very close. They sounded like they came from just the other side of the creek from our campfire. Deb and Dee were sitting side by side and they thought the coo sounded like it was just over their shoulders. Dee got up from her seat and came toward me a bit unsettled. It unnerved Deb and she went to the tent soon after this. To us it sounded as

Fig 4-18 Deb Our Aussie, Keeping Journal

though they were uttered by a young female because of the sweetness and gentleness of its tone.

I did not hear the coo myself because I had stood up to grab some more firewood but I distinctly heard the whoop. As soon as I did I looked to the others who I know were not messing with me. There was absolutely no doubt that what I heard was, "W-H-O-O-O-P", whoop. It was not an owl nor was it a bear because those creatures don't actually speak like this had. We heard back exactly what we had been saying into brush just a few minutes prior.

The next morning Deb, Dee, and I took a walk south along

the road. We got maybe a half mile when Deb started feeling ill. We stopped and she said she felt they didn't want us to go any further and our presence was not welcome. Within moments of her telling us this we began hearing and feeling the gumping noise. I was thrilled because this was the first time I had heard it, but Deb turned back to camp and we couldn't get her to walk any further with us. Dee and I decided to press forward. We got to the bend in the road and got gumped even more. It resonated in our chests and seemed to come from down the slope to our right, west of the road. I counted five to six gumps per burst. Bursts were separated by one to three minutes at a time.

Dee tried to record the sound on her phone but its frequency was too low to register. After several more minutes of this we began to head back toward camp. On the way back we cracked some logs against some tree trunks. We hit them pretty hard and even broke a couple. We would stop every few steps and listen for any responses, but it had quieted down completely. We figured that was probably about all we were going to get so we started walking a bit faster and all we could hear was the gravel beneath our feet and our walking sticks when suddenly we heard a protracted roar howling from the upper ridge above and east of the road. It was so obvious and so strong we both looked at each other wondering if we were actually experiencing it (because these things just don't happen right?).

The roar lasted for about fifteen to twenty seconds and just as it ended Dee looked up to her right and exclaimed, "Oh my God, something is coming down the mountain at us!"

For a split second I could feel her urge to bolt from a fight or flight reaction, but she held her ground and so did I. We just looked at each other frozen and as soon as we did the gumps began directly from behind me from the west. Whatever had been gumping us earlier had followed us, or there were more than one down there. That was when things became very clear in my mind that we were dealing with one too many coincidences to continue avoiding the obvious explanation for what was happening.

After a few moments this all simmered down. We waited a bit longer and then returned to camp. We asked whether anyone had heard anything. They said they didn't and we proceeded to describe what we heard and then we heard three very loud tree knocks, the third was so loud it sounded more like a crash.

When we told Deb what had happened she told us that she had been followed by chest thumping noises both down from the west and from the ridge to the east of the road as she headed back to camp. She finally got so tired of it she audibly told them to leave her alone and go and pester Dee and myself. Well, it seems they did just that. All of this was just too much for my way thinking to be pure happenstance and misidentified sounds.

I asked Thom if there were any animals up there that made that gumping sound. He said there was a bird that made a noise kind of like that but that it started out slow and then increased in frequency before it stopped. What I heard was a fixed frequency and besides birds don't do infrasound that feels like a bass drum in your chest cavity.

Anyway, there were a few other things that happened but I wanted to capture the bulk of what I remember and what I found most significant. I hope one can see why I was so excited about what happened and why this was a life changing event for me. It's not that I didn't believe these people were real, it's just that I very much wanted my own experience with them to help bring it more fully to my scope of reality. I welcome thoughts on what we felt and heard on this my first bigfoot encounter.

Chapter 4-7
22 June 2014 1140

Conclusions

The car was loaded... packed as closely as the first Mars Mission will have to be. Every nook and cranny was filled. There was no small space unoccupied when we realized there were still two garbage bags that had to come with us. Normally we could not have such a large amount of waste, but it seems someone among us was not leaving waste food in the woods for the wee critters nor was all the paper waste being burned as it should have been. All that should have been in the garbage was metal and plastic but, unfortunately, this was not the case.

Eleven days in this camp was ending... sadly ending. I did not wish it so, but my wishes are seldom those that command the day. I had no idea how we were going to get this last bit into the car. There was little enough room for the last two occupants, let alone this added burden. The result was the two passengers had to each carry a garbage sack until we could find a dumpsite to leave our offering. I seemed to recall that I had seen a disposal site just south of Orleans on the highway... a recollection that proved unreliable in the actuation! The result was, our garbage rode with us as far as Weitchepec and the small Convenience Store located there. It was with grateful hearts and sans garbage that we left that tiny store bound for the Bald Hills Road.

As I waited for my people to complete their duties at the store, I walked to the bluff and looked down on the absolutely stunning view of the confluence of the Klamath and Trinity Rivers. I watched as the two waters combined to make one strong flow to the sea. My mind retreated to all that I had watched happen in those days of interaction. There had been fourteen people who had visited our camp... some for but a night... some for the entire time... VIRTUALLY ALL

Figure 4-19 Trinity River (L.) meets Klamath River (R.)

had had an interaction with the large and hairy folk residing there! That in itself was remarkable but what was beyond amazing was that each had done so at their own level of comfort... or, perhaps, discomfort.

I have been interacting with these people for fifty-six years... Arla for about the same period. We have seen many over these years to the point that while it is always exciting to be allowed to

131

view them, we are confident in what we see. It is not a frightful thing nor is it upsetting to us to view them at close range. We have lived with them long enough to understand that they are not violent beings and are not dangerous to us or to anyone who treats them with the respect due them. Of course, any being is going to be dangerous if one is negligent enough to threaten its young or even its person. There isn't a mother on earth worthy of the name mother who will not use whatever force is available to her to defend her children... why would these people be any different? There are other cases where one can put themselves into danger with these large beings, but none that I know of that does not involve disrespect towards them in some manner... usually in the form of threats of physical violence where the sasquatch person feels in danger for their safety.

Others do not have the long years of involvement on which to rely, so are, understandably more prone to fear being generated within themselves. I have been told often of the dangers of fear. These people strive to eliminate it from their encounters and we certainly witnessed that on this extended trip. They have told me innumerable times that, "Fear is the one human emotion we cannot work through. If fear is present, we cannot interact safely with humans." Even with that understanding, it does still happen at times. In our time at the Ronnyvoo, it happened with several of our people.

One such instance was Kathi's case of being frozen in place while the big guy made good his retreat. Kathi was not harmed, nor was she afraid of her guest. Her fear was of her condition. Being locked up like she was had never occurred with her before and she did not know quite how to react to it. Even in her state, she did not express her fear, but merely sought to resolve the situation she had created and to retreat from it gracefully. What I heard when I approached her was not fear of the being, but concern for her condition. Knowing what I did of what happened, I knew she was in no danger and was even able to be a bit flippant with her as she openly voiced her apologies for having created the situation as it then existed.

Another case was Nancy's sighting in her camp after Kathi had asked them to leave her so she could sleep and to visit Nancy and Russ in their camp... a request that did not go unfulfilled... As Nancy sat and watched the big fellow, she uttered, "Please don't scare me... this is so different, I could not take being scared... please don't scare me!" ...so, the big guy just faded back to the tree line and did not pressure her further. In both cases, they acted to preclude fear.

Our visitors from the lower camp, Camp Kimchee, in Willow Creek all felt low levels of fear due to the uniqueness of their situations. Deb was probably the most obvious of these as she had no experience with our fellows as she had joined us here from her home in Australia. Bugs and D'Anne both felt levels of trepidation in their encounters but all were able to control it and work through it. It is important to understand that fear will rise in us from time to time. The key is to keep it at a low level such that it does not impede our reactions nor restrict our interactions. Remember, bravery is not the lack of fear. I have never met a brave man who was not afraid at one point or another. Bravery is acting through the fear and not letting it control the situation. It's okay to be afraid... it is not okay to be out of control with that fear.

The most unique manifestation of the workings of the human mind in times of stress occurred with Jackie and our encounter with the two sasquatch people on the road to camp. Instantly her eyes saw the two and her brain said "BIGFOOT"... then, her logical side stepped in... "No... those two beings standing in front of us were not sasquatch, as your brain, I have no recollection of anything like sasquatch, so we must catalog them in terms that I can recognize... They were two men with rucksacks on... they were not bigfoot with shoulders slouched and backs bowed... that was not feet you saw with the Ostman Pads shining but those men were wearing flip flops... Hairy bodies? No, of course not, I have never seen that much hair on a man... it had to be clothing of some type... since they were exactly the same color, it had to have been a uniform like coverall they were wearing. Oh, they were very fast. But they had to have taken many steps to reach the bank over which they disappeared... of course it wasn't but the two steps you thought you saw..."

In fact, by the time we broke camp on this Sunday morning, that uniform had become a ghillie suit and they were five foot four inch Mexican drug mules carrying packs of illicit drugs to market. In JUNE... before the growing season even began here at this high altitude... an altitude where we had ICE form every night.

In addition, virtually every event caused her mind to retreat to its safe place with the data... Deb's gift of the little car... "Some child was playing with that and left it there..." No children and been within MILES of our camp since we had been there.... people had walked on that log the day before... and I have pictures of that log taken the day prior and there is no car on it... but her mind needed to classify it in terms it understood. Kathi's piece of driftwood firewood they left for her... "Oh, that had to have fallen from the trees above..." Uh... slabs of driftwood don't form on living trees... they form in streams of water... if one tried, one could never land any piece of wood in the position of this one... again, retreat to what your mind understands.

I have seen this reaction in many people in many other places and it is no negative reflection on the person exhibiting it. It is merely what is! I had no problem accepting what I saw that day on the road because my mind has great and enduring experiences with this being. My mind could run back to that which it was familiar and keep the image of sasquatch clear and bright because I have seen them on so many occasions. I rather expected to see one on that road during our stay there... two, however, was a bit more than I expected to see!

I'm not sure if there have been psychological studies done on this phenomenon, I'm sure there must have been, but if there have not, there should be. It is a real and startling event.

Leaving Weitchepec, our next goal was the beauty and grandeur of Redwoods National Park. The drive across the Bald Hills Road to Redwood Creek was uneventful until we arrived into the park to find traffic stopped in the roadway, negating travel while a small bear plied his trade of panhandling for largess along the roadway. We were, of course, detained while he went about his chore of cadging comestibles from the people in the cars held up there by his presence.

After gaining our release from this pint-sized con artist, we proceeded north on Highway 101 until taking the by-way... old Highway 101, actually... through Prairie Creek State Park. I have never been through this particular area without seeing elk and today proved no exception. The first things I spotted were the antlers of a few mature bulls protruding from the tall grasses adjacent to the roadway. It happened that there were several large bulls and a few cows at that place. Since the majority of the cows would now have very new calves, I assumed they would be attendant on them and separate from the bachelor herd we were now witnessing.

These elk are remnants of the once widespread Roosevelt Elk herds that had inhabited the pacific slope of the Cascade Mountains through the coastal range from just north of San Francisco all the way to Vancouver Island in British Columbia, Canada. Today, many smaller bands of this species remain in far northern California while their numbers are high and the herd quite healthy

135

as one moves northward into Oregon and Washington. This wetland, coastal denizen is the largest of the surviving species of the North American elk with a mature bull commonly attaining body weights in the twelve hundred to fourteen hundred pound range as compared to the seven to seven hundred and fifty pounds of his Yellowstone cousins.

Dinner at Crescent City then back into the mountains along the south fork of Smith River out of the tiny town of Gasquet (pronounced Gas Kee). It had been a long and eventful day and we were exceedingly tired. As such, we were in our beds before eight pm and lights were out before the skies were dark!

Of course, morning began early, but it was a learning experience as well. Where we were camped, while not on the road, was nearby and the traffic noise, while not loud, was very distinct. We were able to demonstrate and Jackie able to understand that had those been two PEOPLE on that roadway that day who were not wanting to be seen by anyone, they

Figure 4-20 Loaded Car

would have heard us coming for at least a half mile and would have had ample time to vacate the highway before we got there. This chink in her mental armor began like the crack in the dam that

136

led to its collapse. It was very evident that, even though we were well into the trees, we were further from the road than those two "drug mules" would have been and the cars were quite evident to us as we would have been to them.

As the day progressed and we neared Kathi's home in Coos Bay, Oregon other such items came up and each provided another chink. On our final day we left Kathi's home early in the morning and drove about two hours to meet Sue for breakfast in Eugene, Oregon. During that drive we, Jackie and I, talked about these things... Jackie is quite intelligent and has had a great deal of schooling in the field of psychology so understands exactly what was happening in her mind. By the time we parted at the airport in Portland, she was quite convinced that she had, indeed, had the sighting of a lifetime. It lacked only verification from an independent source. That verification came to her from her longtime friend when he told her of interviewing Yeti witnesses who initially thought they'd seen a man in a coat...

Finally, she realized that her mind did, indeed, play a trick on her and deny her the instant gratification of knowing she'd seen these elusive guys but she will now make up for lost time in her learning about our friends...

Part 5
The Testimony Leading to the Proof

Bob Gimlin Photo by Tom Yamarone, Used with Permission

Chapter 5-1
Common Sense

From the very first, the Patterson-Gimlin Film (PGF) created a storm of controversy. Immediately, there were many people who screamed "hoax" as loudly as their lungs would allow. Although there was no evidence of any hoax, these people were not swayed, they continued. This made me think about this for a bit... and it gave me pause to consider the situation in some more depth...

The film itself I will deal with in more detail in the chapter devoted to it. We will rely heavily on testimony from a very knowledgeable analyst and professional creature and film maker. Now, I'd just like to delve into some common sense concepts and investigate the logic therein.

In 2004, a tabloid journalist published a book meant to be an expose' on the PGF... He invaded the small valley west of Yakima, WA where both Bob and Roger lived and by plying some members of the local community liberally with drink, extracted some tales of the pasts of these two men. And found one man who claimed to have been the man in

Figure 5-1 Greg Long, Author

the suit the day it was filmed. It is a shame that Long didn't spend as much time investigating his puppydog and his relationship with the valley where the film was made, since it turned out he did not even know how to get to the Bluff Creek film site! I will not delve into individual stories here as, at this date, there is no proof, only hearsay, concerning what happened in that tiny community.

One thing that is certain, however, is the testimony of the fellow who claimed to have worn the suit. From his own published

testimony, we gain the following statement from him: "We drove to the area and about four or five miles up the Bluff Creek Road..." ...to a point where we got out and I put on the suit that was made from the hide of a red horse... It was glued to a set of fishing waders on the

Figure 5-2 Bob Heronimous with Suit He Said Was Patty

bottom... the top was put on over my head and I wore football pads to bulk me up more... I walked across the bar one time while Roger filmed me and that was it. I removed the suit and we left and drove home.

At this point, I would like to take a few moments to examine these statements for their logic. Understand, please, I have no way to refute what he has stated here empirically but does it withstand logical examination?

First, I would ask, why Bluff Creek? The film site, and this location has been empirically proven to be correct by experts in their field, is over six hundred miles from the two filmmaker's homes in their tiny valley west of Yakima, WA. It has been stated and universally accepted that Bob and Roger rode together regularly in the Cascade Mountains less than forty miles from Bob's home and even closer to Roger's home. In addition, the pair had been riding as recently before the filming as late August and early September in the Mount Saint Helens area, just west of their homes.

In Roger's 1966 Book on the subject, he chronicles sightings and encounters all over this area of Washington and down into Oregon as well as the Northern California area where the film was shot. Obviously, he knew that there were more encounters in Washington than in any other area as he so stated in his book.

Anyone who has ever attempted any task remotely from his home knows that the further one is from home, the more he must carry with him just to cover "what if" contingencies. It would logical to me that if I were out to perpetrate a hoax, I would choose spot with a relatively high rate of encounters reported or somewhere with a history of sightings. One of the first things I would look for would be a spot, close to my home base, where I could manufacture some evidence that would serve as my reason for being there to begin with, then I would hire someone who knew how to get to the area to be my actor.

Next, I would make sure I had my gear ready and I would get into an adventitious position for filming the scene. It would be absolutely necessary that I anticipate the tests that would be forthcoming on my film, my gear and my methodology to prove it a hoax. After all, what good is a hoaxed piece of film if it is proven a hoax? There are plenty of those available today on Youtube.com.

It must be noted here that it would be utterly impossible to know in 1967 what would be available in 2015 to be used as a tool in vetting a piece of film. Who would even imagine that film in 2015 would be a virtually non-existent commodity and that such scenes as Roger filmed in 1967 would not even be done by actors in suits and make up? It would have been completely impossible for a film maker in 1967 to fool an investigator in 2015 no matter what contrivance he used to do so.

Now, in light of the prior statements, why would anyone preparing a hoax leave the area of their own home, an area that is known to be rich in sasquatch lore to travel over six hundred miles to simply film a hoax?

Heronimous stated that "We drove down there..." I would like to know who the "we" are. Roger and Bob were in California, in the Bluff Creek area conducting investigations in that area and had been the entire month of October. Witnesses placed them, with their horses, etc. in the area. They bought gas and they visited with people such as Al Hodgson in Willow Creek, firmly placing them in the area. If Heronimous had a "we" it must have been someone exclusive of the film.

The film site is not "four or five miles up the Bluff Creek Road" as he stated, it is more than twenty miles of twisting, steep and narrow mountain road just to get to Roger and Bob's base camp at Louse Camp on Notice Creek. From there, it was a three and a half mile hike up bottom of Bluff Creek to the film site. This is not someplace that would be found easily nor accessed without great effort.

Heronimous stated that the suit was made from the hide a red horse (although he later changed that to a black horse) and was made in two parts. The lower part was a pair of fishing waders with the hide glued to it and the upper part was a

Figure 5-3 Patty Rearview

142

slip over which he put on over football pads to make him look beefier. If this were correct, there would have to be a seam where the top piece draped down over the bottom piece.

Careful examination of Figure 5-3 reveals no such dividing line. Further, I have owned many pairs of fishing waders over the years and I have NEVER had one that showed any definition of my leg, arm and back muscles. Figure 5-3 shows all of those very well.

I will leave the fine points of dissention concerning the suit to the chapter where the book and the work of Mr. Bill Munns are discussed in some detail. Here, I am simply questioning the logic of some of the statements made by some of those who have made remarks about the film.

Sometime after Roger's death in January of 1972, a costume maker came forth with the assertion that he had been in negotiation with Roger Patterson to make a bigfoot suit. Phillip Morris was a Halloween costume maker specializing in "off the rack" ape suits that sold for about $495. While he must have made enough of these suits to sustain himself in business, there is no evidence that he ever sold one to Mr. Patterson.

It certainly would not be any great surprise to anyone considering it that someone planning a documentary on the subject might feel they had a need for such a suit to provide background shots for his film. Certainly, just over one minute of film would not be enough to hold the interest of a serious documentary viewer.

Around 1978, Mr. Heronimous appeared with one of Morris's suits. He donned the suit and strutted his version of Patty's walk. Figure 5-2 is a photograph of Heronimous with this suit and Figure 5-4 shows him in the suit. It is most important that this photo be examined very closely because it shows some glaring anomalies that call into question the very possibility of Patty being a suit of any kind, let alone one of Mr. Morris's Halloween Special versions.

Figure 5-4 Heronimous in Morris's Suit

Please take a moment and examine this photo. To me, the first thing that jumps out at me is that it has more folds in it than a fat man's chin! One does not see musculature nor definition of form, simply folds in the material making up the suit! The overlapping of the legs onto the feet is evident and the hands are obviously separate from the material of the arms... the hood of the headpiece quite obviously overlaps the shoulders and bunches up at that point.

144

Did Heronimous ever wear such a suit as an actor in Roger's documentary? I don't know... and, other than Bob Heronimous, no one else now living does either. That he did some acting for Roger prior to or just after the film we know for fact. But, again, that would be no more than consistent with Roger's desire to produce a quality documentary.

He stated that after driving from Yakima, Washington to Bluff Creek, California, a distance of over six hundred miles on two lane road, he donned the suit, walked across the flat while Roger filmed him, removed the suit and drove back home. He stated that Roger shot only one take.

Again, logic begs a huge question. Bob and Roger were in the Bluff Creek area for three weeks. Independent statements have placed them there. They have stated publicly that during that time, they drove the roads at night in Bob Gimlin's one ton stock truck looking for sign and spent their days on horseback, riding and searching. If one knew one had someone coming to do a hoax shoot, why would that one invest all this time in the endeavor? For what POSSIBLE purpose would be served by so doing?

In summary, those who insist this is a hoax would have us believe that, first off, a suit such as that demonstrated by their poster child, Bob Heronimous was what we were actually seeing in the film. This in and of itself is totally ludicrous, but now it gets even worse. According to these people, we are to believe...

1. Roger and Bob left an area rich with sasquatch lore and history of encounters to drive over six hundred miles on two lane highway to...

2. Spend the next three weeks driving all night and riding all day in search of sign...

3. Hike three and a half miles up a creek bed to a pre-arranged spot... it had to be pre-arranged if Heronimous was going to meet them there three weeks after they left Yakima...

4.   Have the actor walk one time across the field and shoot it without even considering a back-up...

5.   Shoot the entire scene on the last twenty-four feet of a hundred foot roll of film after shooting seventy-six feet of Bob and his pack horse...

6.   Shoot if from BEHIND the actor the whole time... always chasing the scene.

7.   Use a suit that had to be VERY expensive that would never be seen again.

It is simply beyond comprehension that an experienced film maker, and Roger was experienced, would set up to film any scene of importance with only the tag end of the roll of film available to him. Film analysis shows that the film began with him running behind the figure he was filming... now, why, logically, would anyone do that? If I were setting up to film a scene and I had control of it, FIRST, I'd start with a fresh roll of film in my camera... certainly, if I wanted to think I was going to fool someone into thinking I was not hoaxing, I'd not have more than a few feet exposed so it would look like it just happened while I was filming the scenery.

Second, I'd be where I could get a decent presentation as my subject traversed the field. Certainly, there would be more than a second or two of face/frontal shots. There is absolutely nothing logical or contrivable about what actually came out on those few hundred frames of film. Nothing is as it would be if a person were to set out to film a hoax. Every part of it just cries out that it happened spontaneously... unexpectedly... all at once!

There is one final nail in the coffin of Mr. Heronimous, Mr. Long and Mr. Morris and that is the simple fact that Bob Heronimous at no more than six feet two inches simply does not FIT into the body of a being more than seven feet four inches tall!

146

The best evidence is empirical evidence… that which can be tested and tried… well, here it is. For all who want empirical evidence to the exclusion of all other forms, please look at Figure 5-5 below…

In this figure, Patty and Bob Heronimous are compared side by side in the same vertical scale. He is something less than six foot two inches and she is between seven feet four and seven feet ten inches as determined by three different methods of anatomical estimations as taken from the film itself. As is evident here, the man

Figure 5-5 Heronimous and Patty Scaled to the Same Scale

on the right will not fit into the suit on the left. Look at his legs… we'd have to move where his knee bends. In addition, we'd need to totally revamp his arms and I'm not even sure how we'd go about using a spine stretcher on him.

No, Bob H… I'm afraid I'm going to have to say you were not the person in a suit imitating a real life sasquatch. The logic simply is not there to support such a wild claim!

147

Chapter 5-2
Tales From the Film

In 2011, The National Geographic Channel aired a documentary on sasquatch in which they engaged one of Hollywood's foremost makeup men, film analysts and "creature creators" to attempt to look at the slightly more than a minute of the Patterson-Gimlin Film and see if it was possible to make some definitive conclusions concerning that film. To effect this, Munns was allowed access to the home of Mrs. Roger

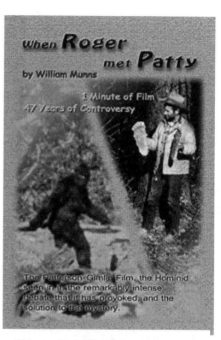

Figure 5-6 The Most Important Book Written on the Subject of the Patterson-Gimlin Film

Patterson where he was given a first generation copy of that famous footage. Since this is the most definitive footage of a sasquatch ever attained, it has been shown over and over and over again, but always with a copy of a copy of a copy, since access to the original film has not been granted in the middle to recent past. Mr. Munns used the latest technology available to stabilize the film and produced a very fine image from a bouncing, blurred effort!

Very simply, Bill determined four major aspects that are immediately visible that precludes this from being film of a man in any kind of a suit:

1. Arms and torso are too long to be a human.
2. Hips are too low to be a human.
3. Upper and lower legs are out of proportion to human.
4. Joints cannot be made to line up with human.
5. In addition, using the reported distance from camera to subject of one-hundred feet, the measured height of the subject on the film to be .0448" and the probable use of a fifteen millimeter lens yields the height of the subject to be seven feet six inches... the height of one in 20,000,000 humans... not likely to be found easily.

These data and conclusions are not hearsay, nor are they the conclusion of unskilled, uneducated, biased persons. These are taken empirically directly from the frames of the film itself by an expert in the field of costuming, makeup and creature making. I don't know what more a sane person would need in order to determine that this was NOT film a man in a suit!

The Film

There are two forms of evidence... The first is anecdotal or eyewitness evidence... what one has seen or found or been told of a factor. The second is empirical evidence... that which can be measured, tested or repeated. This latter is the evidence science requires to prove or disprove a theory. The main reason eye witness or anecdotal evidence is not acceptable while it would be acceptable in a court of law is that there can be no cross examination in our application. Hence, it must either be accepted or not, dependent on any of several factors which may not be the same from person to person.

What we are about to discuss now will be empirical evidence. The film itself supplies this. The testimonies of Roger and Bob, though first hand, are anecdotal. What Heronimous reported is strictly anecdotal. Even my rebuttal of his claims, though logical and reasonable are, mostly, anecdotal. The film, however, supplies measurable, verifiable data. Having all the image data to work with allows us to develop a factual description of what occurred as Roger's camera was running.

In this next section I will be relying heavily on Bill Munns' book. Much of what I report will be quoted directly from that work. As stated, Mr. Munns is an expert in his field and his testimony can be relied on, even in an anecdotal case, but in this section, other than his underlying experience, all will be empirical data.

The film is shot in six segments totaling nine hundred fifty four frames. Each of these segments tells us something about the film in total and even more about the mood of the person filming the incident. It is important that we understand what these segments mean.

Segment One consists of the first ninety-four frames of film. The camera starts while Roger is running forward. Although there have been people try to contest this allegation, as they have protested virtually everything ever said that would tend to help one understand the truth of this film, this is an irrefutable fact base on empirical image data.

If this were a hoax, Roger would have had to position his

150

actor, decide where he would go and where Roger would run to in order to chase after him. He then had to cross the creek and dress his actor, brush the suit out, position him at the starting point, have the actor wait while Roger recrossed the creek to get camera ready. He would then make sure the camera was wound and the critical settings correctly made. Only now could he look to his actor and call for action with only one quarter of a roll of film left in the camera.

Typically, the camera is started then the call for the scene to begin is given. In this case, it would, of necessity, have been a visual signal because creek noise and distance would have made an aural cue impossible. Add to the above factors the fact that the head mask would have added to the problem of making a spoken command a viable option. But, that is not what happened here. Roger was not standing still as the action began. He started the camera while running.

Would a hoaxer have given any thought to whatever difference it would make? Whether he started his camera while running or standing still, who would ever notice? The only possible reason a hoaxer might start his camera while he was moving would be so that he could use it as a "proof" that is not a hoax. However, no one, to my knowledge, has ever mentioned this as a reason to argue for the reality of the film and Roger never brought it up, so why would a person load a gun and not shoot it?

On the contrary, however, a real person encountering something strange, frantic to get off his horse, get his camera out and start filming as soon as he was able to point his camera would start shooting under whatever conditions prevailed, even while still running.

It is unclear, even today, at what speed the Kodak camera Roger used was operating. It was capable of either sixteen frames per second or twenty-four frames per second. Since it is not known

151

which speed setting was being used, that means the ninety-four frames of segment one spanned from four to six seconds.

The camera was switched off at frame ninety-four and back on at frame ninety-five. There is no splice between the two frames and frame ninety-five has the over exposure that is common to the startup of the camera.

Segment Two runs from its beginning at frame ninety-five to frame one hundred ninety. It is coincidence that it is the same length as Segment One also being from four to six seconds in length. In this segment, Patty is sometimes blocked by the foreground and her lower legs are obscured from sight much of the time by the terrain. Roger is still moving forward, chasing her, so it shows her back view.

The film image data shows as an irrefutable fact that from camera shut off of Segment One to startup of Segment Two, Patty continued move in a generally steady direction at a generally steady pace. It is a measureable fact that she took three to four steps in the off time.

I can think of no plausible reason a hoaxer would stop and restart when acting with due deliberation as was done here. It would be entirely plausible, however, for someone who in is the middle of a spontaneous event to have a reason to do so.

Segment Two stopped at frame one hundred and ninety with Roger near the creek, but he has not yet crossed over it.

Segment Three is only two frames in length. Frame one hundred and ninety-one and one hundred and ninety-two are likely a trigger slip. Further, there was no editing done before or after. Again, the film data showed that only a few seconds passed between Segments Two and Three.

If this is a hoax, why would the hoaxer start his film where the creek would be in the way of his progress? Roger was wearing slick-soled cowboy boots which are notorious on slick surfaces, especially on uneven, slick surfaces like rounded stream rocks. Crossing a moving stream is tricky at best and in such footwear, the potential for disaster is tremendous. One slip here and the camera is immersed in water and if that happens, the lights go out and we all go home. Further, as alluded to prior, the stream being between the actor and the camera virtually guarantees no communications between the two.

Figure 5-7 The PGF Film Site

Segment Four begins with frame one hundred and ninety-three and runs for forty frames to number two hundred and thirty-three. This segment has few sharp images because Roger is running around a branch structure and toward Patty as he films with his lens pointed at the ground. By this time, he has crossed the creek and is moving up the bank. This segment is only two to two and a half seconds in length.

The longest single segment and, arguably, the single most important is Segment Five. This begins with frame two hundred and thirty-four and extends to frame six hundred and eighty-six or four hundred and fifty-two frames in length. This provides between nineteen and twenty-nine seconds in time.

Over the years, one of the great arguments promulgated by those who do not believe this film to be real is that Roger purposely moved the camera to intentionally create an indecipherable film to hide the imperfections in the suit. This clip of film refutes that argument totally.

This is where we find the almost universally known "look back" scene. Roger is planted solidly and is not moving for the first time since the film began. The camera is being held steadily and Roger is closer to Patty than at any point in the entire evolution. Roger is doing absolutely everything that a cameraman could do to insure the best images possible. This segment will be the source for some of the best data to come from the entire film.

The final piece, Segment Six is frame six hundred and eighty-seven to frame nine hundred and fifty-four. These two hundred and sixty-seven frames find that Roger has moved to get around trees and Patty is distant from the camera.

The absolutely surest indication of a hoax would be if there were time lapses between the segments of film. It is certain there was no editing, cutting or splicing done on the film as that would be immediately evident to a qualified investigator such as Mr. Munns. Given the data above, it's obvious that if the time between segments is more than a few seconds it would be an indication that time was taken to reset the filming spot or the actor.

The film was never interrupted except as described. The subject never paused in her retreat from the area. It was all one smooth movement by Patty which was filmed in six segments by the cameraman, Roger Patterson. Analysis of the shadows proved the total film was shot in just over a minute total elapsed time.

Would a hoaxer really try to film the entire sequence in one take? Would he try while running to start his camera, stop it and start it again while still on the move? Would he pause, do a two frame trigger slip... cross a creek... start the camera while running up a creek bank incline, charge forward then hold quite still for a perfect Segment Five then go back to running and starting his camera for a wild Segment Six all in under two minutes for about one minute of film? To believe this would be, for me, to press the limits of credulity!

Making the Suit – Practical Considerations

Perhaps the most critical portion of this treatise on the truth of the Patterson-Gimlin Film is the nature of the alleged suit and what it takes to produce such an effect. Because it is so important, I will be relying heavily on the words of one who has made a career of creating such devices. To this end, much of this portion will be directly from the words of Bill Munns and out of his terrific book, "When Roger Met Patty".

To begin with, "The most annoying and worthless ideas are offered by amateurs in the creature design and fabrication field who cannot tell the difference between what is possible and what is practical." To this entire class of people, if it is not totally impossible, it becomes something that is now a viable option to be used to support any argument they wish to put forth. For the person actually walking the walk and not just talking the talk, just because something is possible does not make it viable. It is possible to break a leg... it is possible to run a sub ten second hundred meter race... it is not practical to do so at the same time.

155

It is, today, possible to make a costume such as that suggested by Heronimous, split at the waist with an attached head mask to the upper torso but that is not practical and no one does it that way. Why? Well, for one thing, it would be outrageously hot inside such a contraption and safety would require that the actor be broken out and cooled down periodically. Pulling such a costume off a sweat covered actor would be problematical at best and extremely difficult at the worst. Therefore, though it's possible to do a suit this way, no one in the real world would ever attempt it.

While I don't intend to get into the mechanical difficulties presented in the construction of a suit such as this, I'll leave that to Bill, know, simply, that they are rampant. Suffice it to say for our purposes here, at this time, as John Chambers, Reuben Steindorff and others of the day have said... it would have been impossible to create a suit that did all that creature did at that time in history! Just the head turn and look back would have created virtually insurmountable problems and challenges to a person making such a costume with the non-stretch fur of the day.

Just the fitting of the actor would have presented problems to an amateur such as Roger. There would be an initial fitting session where the actor's body would have to be molded or some other process to construct a manikin on which to build and form suit padding and, ultimately, the suit itself. The process would, according to the experts, require a minimum of five or six fitting sessions during fabrication.

Breast Movement

We have all done it... when walking, our eyes are not on where our feet are going and, suddenly, we find the ground is not where we expected it to be. Perhaps it is only an inch or so lower, but the result is that when our foot does land, finally, our body jars a bit and a minor shock wave is sent over it. Invariably, we feel a quiver in our tissues.

156

Remarkably, this happened with Patty as well during the lookback phase. Her attention was back on Roger and Bob as her foot stepped forward and down and the ground was a bit further away than her mind had processed it to be. The result was, her boob jiggled!

When this phenomenon was observed in the film, and it took a frame by frame, stop action analysis to observe it, it caused questions to arise as to whether it would even be possible to achieve this effect in a suit. To this end, Mr. Munns applied for and received a research grant to investigate what it would take to reproduce this.

Figure 5-8 Katherine Ross

In his research project, he tested the products used to make prosthetic breasts in the era of the mid to late 1960s such as was used for the actress Katherine Ross in the film "The Stepford Wives" and compared their mobility and fluidity to the breast of live female models.

Mr. Munns hypothesis that it would take a natural fluidity to allow the breast to actually flatten vertically and broaden horizontally as was exhibited by the Patty figure in the PGF itself was tested under controlled circumstances with the materials available.

He chose three separate materials that had been used virtually exclusively in that era to create these prostheses and found that in all cases, NO fluidity was possible. In all three cases, the material was too rigid to allow motion under the natural forces shown to exist in the PGF. It was only when live models where subjected to those same forces that the ripple effect allowed by the natural fluidity of the breast was observed.

Today, there are new and improved materials that are used to create these prostheses, but that was in 1967, not today. In that era, no such material existed that was in practical use which would allow the observed jiggle.

Roger an Artist?

An argument put forth by some nay-sayers states that since Roger Patterson was an artist and saddle maker, he could certainly make a suit... "To expect Roger to be able to make a suit because he was artistic and could build a saddle is utter and laughable fantasy... a delusional monument to wishful thinking!" There is no evidence that would suggest that Roger ever built or modified any suit, before or since that 1967 time, so are we to believe he did what the best in Hollywood could not do and that he did it on his first try?

Those stating "Of course Roger could build that..." have absolutely none of the qualifications necessary to make that judgement but pull it out of thin air and expect us to believe them without question... fascinating! "There is simply no reasonable expectation that a person who has sculpted figurines or done some sketches is also, automatically, a natural to build a complex creature suit." (Munns, "When Roger Met Patty")

Head Shape and Size

When crafting a creature suit, especially the head, there is a cardinal rule... the suit can only add to the person wearing it, it cannot take anything away. This is something that is difficult to accept for the non-knowing and is a source of confusion and has been to the expert, often, from day one.

Apes have a head that goes BACK from the brow ridge while humans have a skull that goes UP from the brow ridge... what this really means is, a human head simply will not fit inside even a gorilla's head. Even a cursory glance at Figure 5-9 will convince most people

Figure 5-9 Gorilla

that if one compares the distance from the brow ridge to the forward crown of the head, the distance is just too slight to allow a human head to fit there.

To make ape suits to accommodate humans, the head has to be made larger than life or the human head simply will not fit in it. In order for a person to see out the eye apertures and to breathe that crown must be extended vertically. In fact, when Mr. Munns attempted to create a mask similar to what it would have taken to simulate Patty, using the dimensions of the figure in the film, a human head WOULD NOT FIT! Attempts to alter the mask to fit the human head resulted in bad slippage and vision was a real problem. Further, the inability to maintain the nostrils where the actor's nose would be became very problematical and breathing was virtually not possible while the mask was being worn.

Figure 5-10 Suit Showing Folds of Neck Material

In the words of Bill Munns, "Anyone advocating (the film as being) a hoax can simply remove these concerns by making a mask that does have the shape and size of the head relative to the body and letting an actor wear it and film this and show us... No one has ever done it."

Neck

The neck in suits has always been the most difficult area to make look and lay correctly if any head movement is necessary by the subject. These myriad problems were greatly magnified in the era of this film before the advent of stretch materials. It is enough to make one wonder, with all the problems that confronted suit makers with the neck, how did Patty manage to have a smooth, flowing neck before the look back, an unwrinkled neck during the head motion and a smooth and sleek neck after it was complete when she resumes her forward eye direction and we have an excellent view of her back? "The neck simply does not do what costume necks did in that time, with the materials of that era."

Breasts

To analyze breast motion required more knowledge of photo

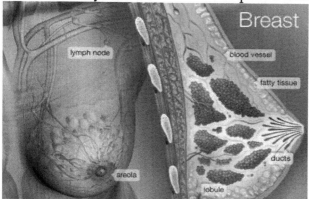

manipulation than I have even as a former professional photographer and is certainly more technical than we need for our purposes here. Again, I refer the reader with a desire for a more in-depth

Figure 5-11 Anatomy of a Human Breast

discussion of these aspects of this phase to Bill's excellent book. The most important point is that the process allowed identification of breast movement in Patty.

As Patty looked back at the camera, her right leg is stepping forward and, when it tries to touch down, the ground is not there. It is just a bit lower than her brain believes it will be and, hence, her walk cycle is expecting it to be, causing a hard step. The step sends a shock wave up her torso and the breast jiggles... compresses vertically and expands horizontally.

In order to understand this anomaly better, Mr. Munns applied for and received a grant to finance an academic study of the phenomenon. In this study, he proposed to use the three methods to produce prosthetic breast in the mid-1960s and utilized the services of female models for comparison and confirmation. In a nutshell, what Bill found was that none of the materials used in the day allowed for the movement observed. The only configuration that produced the compression and expansion observed in the Patty figure were real, live female breasts on the living models participating in the study.

For those wanting scientific proof, there it is... a verifiable, repeatable scientific study that offered proof that the observed jiggle could not have been possible in a prosthetic breast manufactured in 1967. In Bill Munns own words, "...Even ten years after Roger's film, we can't find a single verifiable example of a fluid filled prosthetic that actually imparted a visually verifiable fluid motion to a costume."

If the breast jiggle was not producible by an artificial means, but only by an actual female breast, what does that say for the theory that this is a person in an ape suit? If it is not a person in an ape suit, what is it?

Skin Shifts

Another anomaly occurs during the "look back" phase of the film that adds more evidence. If one is careful in watching the markings and patterns on Patty's body as she looks back we will see a shift in the hair patterns as the leg extends forward. Research has shown this is a real event. The skin stretches almost all the way up

161

her side to her armpit as the leg extends… Can we achieve this in a costume?

Costume research testing has not produced any such effect. Actually, the exact opposite was observed. When a flexible material such as the fur would have to be is shifted against a more rigid material like the glued overlap onto a prosthetic a deformation in the form of a wrinkle appears.

The standard fur cloth from the 1960s and real fur pelts will not exhibit the shifting apparent in the film.

Again, in Bill's words, "…My experiments produced results that would conclude Patty is not a costume… So I personally don't have confidence that a costume can be designed with 1967 type materials and produce this skin shifting effect."

The Back Contours

Before discussing the significance of the back display in the film, there are some things that must be made clear. To that end, I will take a few moments to describe the fur cloth in use by costumers in the mid-60s.

Fur cloth is a woven material that closely resembles a carpet in how it is made. It has a base material and a pile which is the hair fibers interwoven into the base. While the base may be a fiber type material, the pile is normally a synthetic fiber. The base is normally dense to hold the pile solidly in place. This density plus the non-elastic nature of the base which has no elasticity in the direction of the weave either horizontal or vertical and virtually no ability to stretch on the bias, or diagonal, of the weave causes the fabric to, with the slightest stretch on one diagonal of the bias, have compression along the opposite diagonal. In simple terms, if it's pulled one way, it will hump up the other way… it HAS to do it… it has no other choice!

Add to the above, fur cloth has a hair lay. The hair fibers do not stick straight out from the base but lay in one direction or the other. Almost without exception, they were woven so the hair lay tended to align with the vertical weave of the base. This fact becomes important when we join the pieces of the fur cloth so one rides over the other. We must get the hair lay to flow over the seam that joined the two pieces. Just like laying a carpet in one's home, this direction of lay MUST be addressed in the manufacture of a suit.

There have been times in the past when actual animal pelts have been used in the manufacture of suits, and, of course, we are all familiar the use of pelts in the taxidermy field. In this case, the hide is wetted thoroughly, making it somewhat elastic and quite flexible and, while in this condition, it is stretched over a form and glued to that form with pins holding it in the compound curves and in the concave folds of the body until the glue is dried. If it is not pinned, it will drum over those concave curves. The edges of the hide are then carefully stitched. The hair is groomed while the hide is wet and then the hair holds that groomed lay when the piece dries.

People making suits do none of this. There is no rigid body to pull the hide over and around. It is impossible to pin it to concave curves and the cross stitch used to sew the mount would open up when the fur shape flexes.

The creature maker must still follow cloth tailoring procedures while patterning the hide or fabric to the compound curves and joining the edges with glued cloth gussets for a really tight and smooth connection with a perfect hair lay. Whether using fur cloth or real fur hides, the tailoring is the same. Further, real hides that are tanned and dried don't have any elasticity like they do when wet.

The relevance to the back contours is that they represent compound curves and neither standard fur cloth nor tanned pelts will drape over a compound curve without being tailored to that contour. The random folding that occurs with loose fur cloth when there is motion distorting the support will not take compound curves the way tailored cloth can be shaped. This means we can distinguish between random cloth folds and tailored compound curves.

Fig 5-12 Patty from Rear

Patty's back has multiple compound curves that simply won't occur through random cloth folding. Therefore, it must be conceded, if she is a man a suit, that these were designed and tailored to her curvatures. These are contours that occur naturally in anatomy that is aged, overweight and not physically toned. They look "flabby." To argue for a costume, one must then argue that a deliberate and time-intensive effort was made to produce a costume of a flabby bigfoot creature. Roger Patterson spent four plus years passionately striving to convince the world the filmed subject was real, yet these features could not exist in a suit unless he deliberately put them there.

164

Tests were run on the frames to compare the lines on a real back with a costume and those to the lines seen on Patty's back as seen in the film. None of the costume folds resemble the real back contour or Patty's back contours.

Also seen in figure 5-12 is the inverted tee… a vertical line down the spine in the lower back area meeting a horizontal fold across the low waist section. In real anatomy we see this, but it doesn't occur in costumes unless it is specifically tailored into

Fig 5-13 Football Jersey from Back

the design of the costume. This inverted tee would be impossible in a costume unless the material was glued to the person's body inside the suit. Since Bob Heronimous said he merely pulled it on over his head and draped the top half over the football pads he was wearing for bulk, we have to assume it was not so glued. As can be seen that a shirt over football pads do NOT show the inverted tee.

"In consideration of all these individual aspects of the body and the theory and practice of fur costume design in 1967, Patty represents a figure that simply defies just about all the techniques, processes and design concepts of costumes. So the only hope of explaining Patty as a costume is to somehow try to figure out a design so unique and unconventional that the maker was a genius of an order of magnitude the profession has never seen." Bill Munns – "When Roger Met Patty"

165

Real Life Biology, Morphology and Anatomy

In the preceding section, we have investigated the possibilities of the subject in the film in light of the needs and restraints of a costume. I believe we have shown that possibility to be seriously lacking in credibility and, in fact, it was shown to have so many serious flaws as to render the possibility of it being a suit to be very nearly impossible.

In this section, we shall look at the morphology of the primate body as compared to the subject of the film under investigation and see if we can determine any areas of concern. Certainly, if we were to identify a characteristic on the subject that is not anatomically possible or probable, that would be cause to suspect a hoax of some sort, wouldn't it? Is what we see in the film a biological reality?

The first thing that must be understood when speaking of the biological realities of a body is that we cannot expect the media projected "centerfold quality" body. Young, toned and physically well-proportioned bodies are not the norm in nature. What we expect to see in the world outside of the media are bodies that are aged, wrinkled to some degree and show adipose (fat) deposits. It is important in any study of Patty to consider only real, honest bodies because, if she is biologically real, her body would not be perfect.

Another consideration of performance is to realize that our perceptions have been altered to the point that adipose tissue is considered undesirable. Our media has brainwashed an unthinking public to a belief that a healthy body doesn't have fat on it. Virtually all body conditioning is designed to reduce or eliminate body fat.

In nature, there is no conflict between muscular

development and fat accumulation. They serve separate functions and both are necessary for survival. The muscle development allows for all the physical movements necessary to live a vigorous, physical, outdoor lifestyle. The accumulation of body fat is food in reserve for those times when food is scarce. In the real world, a powerfully muscled body can and does coexist with healthy levels of stored adipose.

It is common for creatures living in the world to "bulk up" as the end of fall transitions into winter. Also, there is a tendency for females bearing children in non media-driven societies to carry more adipose tissue as a hedge against the exigencies of growing, birthing and feeding of infants. Remember that the PGF was shot in late October, just at the onset of winter. Basically, this means that accumulations of body fat which would tend to obscure most of the musculature are to be expected. It is important that we understand this because there are traits of each that occur in her body.

Head

Although the head shape is not similar to a modern human's it has striking similarities to ancient hominids. It is, in fact, especially reminiscent of Paranthropus boisei, a million year old ancestor who lived in the Olduvai Gorge region of Kenya, Africa. The skull discovered here by anthropologist Louis Leakey is a prime example. It has the same cranium drift back from the brows as exhibited by Patty's head. It also has the suggestion of a sagittal crest which would

Fig 12-14 Paranthropus boisei Skull

have the fleshed out head to have a tapered or pointed rear crown. The facts here do not support any argument of the head shape being false or biologically unreal and is perfectly consistent with reality.

Neck and Back

Examination of the figure in the frames of the film show a very well developed trapezius muscle set, particularly in the upper area. This results in the appearance of a minimized neck. This is very evident in the back views.

In studying the inverted tee, the occurrences in human bodies was consistent and continuing but never occurred in a costume.

On some body builders in certain poses, there was a furrow up the spinal column from the waist to mid torso that ceased there as the skin drummed over the upper back with no spinal furrow then evident. In a funded, scientific study, a very athletically toned woman who was not on the same level as a world-class body builder but was very trim nonetheless was photographed through poses of the back and arms. With her shoulders back, the furrow was all the way up the spine, but as the shoulders rolled forward, the furrow remained in the lower back but the trapezius muscles caused the skin to drum over the spine in the upper back, erasing the furrow in the upper back and to the neck. This study verified the furrow as seen on Patty's back

This is a very subtle detail, one easily overlooked or ignored but is wholly consistent with proper anatomy. It is something that no one would ever design into a suit because it is patently foolish to create something that would only be found with a specific posture and would not occur in any other body position. The effect is that it causes the actor to have to remain in that ONE posture or it will look totally unnatural.

This feature is not something that can occur in a costume by accident. It would require deliberate planning and execution. To place this into a costume, one would have to understand the anatomical conditions necessary to produce such a furrow and we'd still run the chance of it being mistaken for a zipper line. It would be necessary to instruct the anatomist and scientific types on why it suggests a real body and if one knew the anatomical conditions necessary to create it, he would shy from ever using it because of the limited posture, slumped at the shoulders, required by the actor.

Again, quoting Bill Munns… "…The feature is real and occurs on bodies with well-developed trapezius muscles and he shoulders rolled forward somewhat."

Patty had this. Obviously, her lifestyle is physically active and muscle development would be a natural outcome of this. She would spend a great deal of time lifting, moving and placing items of considerable weight. This dead-lifting action is what develops the trapezius muscle.

It should be noted that there are other fatty structures evident on Patty such as pockets of fat under the arms. These do occur in humans who have a substantial amount of fat. The scientific paper generated from this study on Adipose Tissue describes them in detail. Because the filming was in October, Patty would have to be bulked up with reserves of adipose tissue as winter approached.

Breasts

Since we devoted so much time to this subject in the last section, I will just summarize the findings here. We probably went a bit beyond the scope of what should have, strictly, been done in addressing suits, but what is done is done, so we will not repeat it here.

Examination showed Patty's breasts to have fluid motion as was documented and described in the look back segment of the film. Her motion does correspond with the actual dynamics of the body moving on rough ground. The motions seen in the film are what we would expect and find in real breast tissues motion studies. Prosthetic breasts made from any of the materials used for that purpose in the era of the film failed completely to demonstrate motion dynamics.

These studies showed Patty's breasts to be remarkable in their authenticity as compared to real breasts. Her breasts excel when compared to any documented effort in special effects.

Critics have attempted to use the presence of hair on the breasts as a basis for crying hoax. What they fail to understand is that human females have hair on breasts as well, but it is a very fine and nearly colorless velus hair that covers most of our bodies. The follicles are there and could become active and produce more vigorous hair growth and color. Relative to the hair seen on Patty's arms and back the breasts and the chest wall have more of a smooth skin tone, suggesting that hair growth here is modest as compared to the rest of her body. There is nothing about the breasts that is anatomically invalid or false.

"There is nothing about the breasts that can be used to argue for a costume and hoax, but there is strong motion dynamic evidence arguing for real tissue and not prosthetic costume fabrication." Wm. Munns, "When Roger Met Patty"

Hip and Pelvic Lines

One area that critics have attacked mercilessly as proof-positive of a costume is the hip and pelvic lines. An examination of real anatomy reveals the truth of the matter and lays these assertions to waste with little effort. The same arching hip line seen on Patty that has been attributed to a two-piece suit does occur naturally in human hips.

There is a backward diagonal line which would serve no purpose in a costume but does match human anatomy. Also, there

170

is a notch of fur on Patty which defies reason as a costume feature but is found in a similar position on the human body in the form of a curious dimple some people exhibit if they have the proper amount of body fat. Therefore, claims by persons that these prove a costume are in grievous error and are reflecting their own ignorance of human anatomy.

Calf Muscle

Another awkward but not impossible feature in a suit that is seen in Patty is her dynamic calf muscles and the overall shape of that calf. Her calf muscles are highly realistic and such realism is seldom to never seen in a costume. The costume in figure 5-15 (R) is more typical with the only thing showing being the folds in the material from which the costume was made. A search of the archives of costumery failed to yield a single example of

Fig 5-15 Patty's Muscular Calf (L) vs. Suit (R)

such musculature, but human anatomy is rife with examples of this common feature.

Thigh Subduction

Skeptics often lay claim to the "fact" that Patty's thigh subducts under her buttock as a sign of a costume but, in fact, this is simply not true. Scientifically run, monitored and reported tests have shown that in cases where there is more than an average amount of adipose tissue on the buttocks, the upper thigh can and does ride up under the buttocks to a marked degree. I don't think anyone would argue the fact that Patty is not lacking in "Booty" in any form!

Feet

Without doubt, the largest body of evidence supporting the existence of this being is the myriad of footprints left to be found by alert investigators. Unfortunately, these large tracks are also the most commonly forged item of evidence as well. Beginning with construction boss Ray Wallace's tracks have been created with the idea of either spoofing those who would be searching for evidence or actively thwarting the efforts of those people. Just as Wallace created and left tracks in order to calm his crew and allow him to better keep his workers on the job, others have created tracks that were quite obviously fake and easily found in order that, when found,

Fig 5-16 Roger Patterson with Casts of Patty's Tracks

they could "prove" that all reports of such tracks are false because theirs was! Timber companies I have known have used this ploy to keep government from enacting restrictive rules of operation to protect the big people.

Recently, there was a special on National Geographic Channel in which Autumn Williams, former hostess of a show

Fig 5-17 Fake Print

on the Outdoor Channel, escorted a team of science-types into the Cascade Mountains of Oregon. The goal was to locate a sasquatch and film it. Although this goal was not met, evidence was found and the show was pleasant in itself. There was, as usual, the token skeptic from New York who was convinced he could don wooden feet of sixteen inch length and six to seven inches wide and fool every one there... and set out to prove it.

There are some physical and physics facts (phacts?) of life that this young man and others of this ilk forgot to consider before launching this endeavor. Many years ago on Washington's Olympic Peninsula, I was hiking in to a site where a bridge was proposed. I had been contracted by the company who owned the land to do the engineering for his bridge. The hike in was considerable and about halfway to my goal I walked face to face with a large, male sasquatch who was busily eating berries. The soil was very wet as I had waited until this day for the floodwaters from recent heavy rains to retreat back into their banks. This left the soil very soggy and where this particular fellow walked left very deep, very clear impressions. I took time to measure his tracks minutely, including his stride and step, his foot length and width as well as the depth of his tracks.

I then removed my own boots and walked the same route and repeated the exercises with my own tracks.

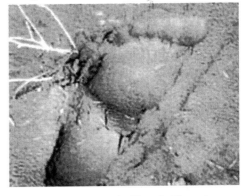

Fig 5-18 Patty's Track Showing Midtarsal Break

When I returned to my office (the desk under the stairs at home where I could escape the antics of a batch of active kids!) I used my planimeter and measured the area of his foot and my own. I determined that

173

my foot covered thirty-four square inches while his foot covered eighty-seven square inches. Using these figures, my weight and his estimated weight and some advanced math, I have learned that when they place their foot flat on the ground before the mid tarsal

break comes into play and are on one foot, they are putting seven and a half pounds per square inch pressure on the ground.

The New York kid on that show was substantially smaller than I am and would have a smaller foot, I am sure, but for the sake of argument let us assume the same size of

Fig 5-19 Roger Casting Track at Bluff Creek

foot so that we know we are dealing with maximums and minimums. I would estimate the fellow's weight at a hundred and seventy pounds therefore; his ground pressure was exactly five pounds per square inch. When he donned his new "feet", he was now covering almost exactly three times as much area without any increase in weight meaning that the ground pressure he could exert was reduced from five psi to approximately one point six psi... and he found what everyone else found who had done this before... he didn't leave any tracks!!!!

It was a real problem trying to walk in the oversized "feet" without falling on his face and he could not leave substantial tracks... two problems with faking tracks. This is why, when fakes are found they are in areas where the soil will allow such alien tracks to actually show.

At Bluff Creek, this was not in evidence. The gravel/sand bar on the creek was firm but not rigid. It would take a track but not easily. There was a vivid trackway left by Patty as she departed and, if I may interject a bit of testimonial evidence here, this trackway was witnessed by several individuals including the principals themselves, Roger Patterson and Bob Gimlin who made castings of the tracks. Also witnessing and attesting to the scene were Al Hodgson of Willow Creek, CA, Bob Titmus of Redding, CA, Rene Dahinden and John Green of British Columbia, Canada. Bob Gimlin told me personally that he climbed up onto a stump and jumped to land beside the track left and he could not sink as deeply as she did. Also, he stated, the horses that weighed between twelve and fifteen hundred pounds did not impress as deeply as she did.

The first thing that must be stressed is that these large

Fig 5-21 Sasquatch Footprints

people are not exactly like us. Their foot morphology and

Fig 5-20 Human Footprints

step mechanics are totally different from ours. When we walk, we, essentially, pole vault over our knees and hips, landing heavily on our heel which will leave a track that is deeper at the heel and will show our arch quite clearly. As we rock forward to begin the next step, ground pressure again increases as the area of the foot on the ground decreases, so the ball of the foot leaves a deeper impression than does the middle part of the foot. Notice also, as shown in Figure 5-20, the alternate, left right orientation of the prints. This is a noted human trait documented in scientific studies.

The sasquatch trackway shown in Figure 5-21 shows the

more inline orientation of their feet when the walk. Also, their step mechanic is significantly different from a human's step. When their foot rises from the ground, it is swung out and then forward with a much higher angle of lift to the foot. This angle is consistently fifty-three degrees in humans and is seventy-four degrees in sasquatch. As the foot swings forward into its landing position directly in front of the foot currently on the ground, it lands in a flat footed manner. This distributes the weight evenly across the entire foot and there is now heavy heel strike as ours show.

As he rocks forward to begin another step, another difference in foot morphology shows... his transverse arch, a hinge in the middle of the foot running across the longitudinal axis of the foot, breaks, allowing his heel to lift while the entire front half of the foot remains in solid contact with the ground. This reduces the effective area of foot on the ground by approximately forty percent, meaning that his psi ground pressure increases commensurately, yielding a track that is penetrated deeper at the front than at the rear. If one views the track cast from a side view, this deeper forward penetration becomes very evident. If it does not, then there may be an attempt to deceive at play here, although the base medium in which the creature stepped may restrict showing this aspect.

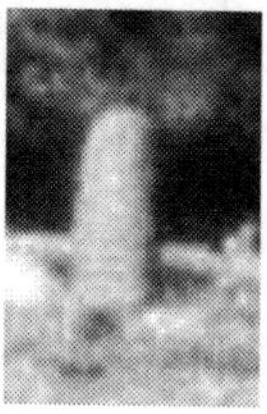

Fig 5-22
Patty's
Foot

Sasquatch have very well developed pads on the bottoms of their feet. These are known as Ostman Pads and are prevalent in any individual, even humans, when they live their lives without shoes. Frame 72 of the film shows these pads very well.

One of the most ludicrous attempts to discredit the film on the basis of footprints and foot morphology came in a television special on the subject of sasquatch wherein a professor of Anatomy from a large New York University stated, on air, that the casts presented him purportedly of the creature had to be fake because he had "...examined them and they were all different. If they were made by the same individual, there would be no differences in the casts..." Excuse, me, but that is the biggest pile of rubbish I've ever heard generated from a supposedly learned man. It is beyond obvious that he may know anatomy, but he knows NOTHING about tracking. As a lifelong hunter and tracker, if I ever found a trackway where there were NOT differences in the appearances of the tracks, I would be highly suspicious!

Beings, when they walk, step differently at different times. The soil medium into which they are stepping varies from one track to the next, sometimes only minutely, but often greatly! The result is, obviously, each track is going to be unique. Yes, there may be, probably will be, great similarities from track to track, but they will never be identical!

Conclusions

Bluff Creek, California

In Conclusion...

From Jerry Crew in 1958 to Thom Cantrall in 2014, the history and controversies of this small microcosm of life in the northwest corner of California abound. In this short treatise we have attempted to encapsulate the arguments against the veracity of this short film we call Patterson-Gimlin.

Of course, it is always easy to ignore facts and make up scenaria that fit the situation that needs support but this is usually done at the expense of the truth and normally has to ignore any number of inconvenient facts. Generally, the first action of the skeptic and doubter is to attack the messenger. To that end, do not ever allow any form of the backstory... who Roger Patterson was or what he did, ever enter into the argument. It is totally immaterial to the point of the validity of this film.

Aside from the empirical facts presented here, there are certain logical arguments that have been presented that defy common sense if one were to wish to perpetrate a hoax. Why would two men haul three horses and all their equipment over six hundred miles from Ahtanum, Washington to Bluff Creek, California then have a third man make the same drive three weeks later to then hike three and a half miles up a creek without trails to expose twenty-four feet of film on the tag end of a spool? Why

179

would one not do that close to one's own home?

The alleged actor's story just has no merit whatsoever. He could not then, nor not since been able to produce a suit that is in any way similar to what we see in the film. There is no way he could fit into any suit the size of what would be required to create a creature he size of the one seen in the film.

Indeed, when all the facts are examined and the hearsay and anecdotes are considered in their true light, the fact becomes very clear that Roger Patterson and Bob Gimlin teamed up to obtain just about a minute of film of a real and living creature that lives wild in the remote places in our country.

While anecdotal evidence is admitted in a civil law case, it is not heeded much in a criminal court. Eye-witness testimony carries more weight than anecdotal evidence, but both suffer the frailty of being reliant on memory and mood of the ones reporting their versions of an incident and both are totally useless if not subject to cross examination and both are totally overridden by empirical evidence. In this volume we have attempted present a clear case of empirical and testable evidence and have pretty much ignored the lesser forms. Hence, there is no personal testimony presented to make this case... there are no statements pro or con about the principals except as exposed by the empirical testing.

The conclusions of this testing of evidence and gathering of facts leads to a conclusion that vindicates those who have gone through so much to present facts that many people do not want to know for one reason or another, but the logical conclusion is, Roger Patterson and Bob Gimlin did, in fact, from 30 September, 1967 to 20 October, 1967... *Spend 21 Days to Destiny!*

Bibliography

"When Roger Met Patty"   Wm. Munns

"Sasquatch-The Search for a New Man"   Thom Cantrall

"Edges of Science"   Thom Powell

"Forest Friends of the Night"   Keith Bearden

"My Journey Into Myth and Mystery"   KJ Blount

"Abominable Snowman"   Ivan Sanderson

Website Postings

http://www.ghostsofrubyridge.com/elk-meadows-ronnyvoo-2014/elk-meadows-ronnyvoo-camp-life/

http://www.ghostsofrubyridge.com/essays/bluff-creek/

Magazine Articles

True Magazine Dec 1959 Dr. Ivan T. Sanderson

True Magazine Mar 1960 Dr. Ivan T. Sanderson

True Magazine Nov 1961 Dr. Ivan T. Sanderson

Argosy Magazine Feb 1968 Dr. Ivan T. Sanderson

Argosy Magazine Aug 1968 Dr. Ivan T. Sanderson

Newspaper Articles

S.F. Chronicle 16 Oct 1958	Bill Chambers, Writer
Humboldt Times 21 Sep 1958	Andrew Genzoli
Humboldt Times 6 Oct 1958	Andrew Genzoli
Houston Post 1960	James Holley

Made in the USA
Middletown, DE
22 July 2016